FINDING
JUSTICE
FOR BONNIE

PATTY PASCIUTO

Copyright © Year 2025.

All Rights Reserved by **Patty Pasciuto.**

No part of this publication may be reproduced in any form, or by any means, electronic or mechanical, including photocopying, recording, or any information browsing, storage, or retrieval system, without permission in writing from Patty Pasciuto.

ISBN

Hardcover: 979-8-90190-014-7

Paperback: 979-8-90190-013-0

Dedicated

Dedicated to my daughter, Bonnie, in the hope of finding the justice she sought and still desires, and to my husband, who worked tirelessly to achieve justice.

Acknowledgement

I thank God for the inspiration to write this book. He will guide you in all that is right.

About the Author

Patricia Bickel spent over 30 years in the field of education. A graduate of the University of Florida, she earned a master's degree from NOVA Southeastern University, specializing in various exceptionalities. She was active in her church, serving as a leader in both the children's program and the adult women's program. She was also an active member of a not-for-profit organization, serving as the president of the board of directors, and she taught horticulture classes for children.

She is the mother of six children who have given her eighteen grandchildren.

Robert J. Pasciuto spent twenty-three years in the United States Navy and earned the rank of Master Chief (MMCM). He did not hold a college degree; however, he attended various military schools, including the nuclear-powered school in New York. He served briefly as a military police officer in Orlando, Florida. He was loved and respected by everyone. He worked as a consulting engineer, mostly as a self-employed individual, for about thirty-five years, where he was sought after for his ability to solve problems and manage the jobs he was given professionally, especially in maintaining operational equipment for companies, mainly in the nuclear-powered industry. He and Patty were married for fifty-six years before he passed away.

Table of Contents

Dedicated i

Acknowledgement ii

About the Author...iii

Chapter One: The Stumbling Block 1

Chapter Two: The Start of Lies 10

Chapter Three: Trying to Find the Truth 24

Chapter Four: What Gives What Takes...................................33

Chapter Five: More Facts...37

Chapter Six: More Deceptions...49

Chapter Seven: Our Son and His Wife.....................................62

Chapter Eight: What We Were Ruled to Believe 65

Chapter Nine: Bonnie's Clues..74

Chapter Ten: The Murder Trial Or Travesty of Justice 79

Chapter Eleven: Life Went On 85

Chapter Twelve: Acquiring More Information.........................90

Chapter One:
The Stumbling Block

"Injustice anywhere is a threat to justice everywhere."

Martin Luther King

If you have never been around a crazy block before, knowing what steps to take can be difficult. Many obstacles can trip you up. Experiences that have happened to you that you wish you could go back and change what you said or did to change the outcome. You cannot go back and correct or change the decisions you made. You must move forward and do your best with what the world has to offer. Pray harder for the Lord to help you do better and listen to what He wants you to do.

It was a typical day on January 7, 1993. It was warm for January. My daughter, Ginny, and I were at the school where I worked and she was taught. I was in my classroom when I was told I had a phone call. It took me by surprise. I did not usually have calls at school. I went to the office to take the call. It was my son-in-law, Mike. What! He explained that my daughter's purse was found in a dumpster that morning. Evidently, she and Mike had argued the night before, and she left around eleven o'clock. He stated that when she did not come back after a few hours, he went to look for her. His mother came over to watch their son. He came to my house and did not see her car, and could not find her vehicle anywhere where he might expect her to be.

The police called him to the motel where the purse was found. They then asked him to come to the police station. Mike said he was still at the police station. They seem to believe I did something to Bonnie. He stated that he did not know where she was or what had happened to her. He asked me if I knew where she was. I told him that I did not. I asked him to call me if she returned, and that I was sure she would return shortly. I did not know what to do or what to think.

I was nervous and prayed that she was safe. It was difficult for me to continue to work; however, I thought that if there were an indication that Bonnie had met a dangerous situation, they would contact me. Working made it easier not to panic and scream. This did not happen to people like me! We were hard-working middle-class Christians.

I worked the after-school program that day. Since I had not heard from Mike or the police, I was unsure what to think or how to prepare myself. I decided to tell Ginny that Bonnie had disappeared. I did not want her to be upset or panic if the police were at the house when we arrived home. Well, the police were not there, nor was Mike. Maybe there was no reason to overreact.

A friend, Linda Marie, was staying with me while her husband was in another state at a new job, looking for a place for them to live. She was watching the news. There it was on the news. The newscasters were at Bonnie and Mike's house, even stating that the police felt there was foul play and that Mike may have played a part in her disappearance. I could not believe it. How could the police not contact me? I could not believe this. I did not know what to do. My husband was working in another state on a project for a few months, coming home every few weeks. I did not know whether to call him, wait to see if Bonnie came home, or wait to see if the police contacted me. I decided to call my bishop (my pastor) to find out if I needed to call my husband. I knew I should, but I hoped he would calm my troubled heart. We decided I should call my husband, no matter what the outcome.

Linda Marie worked off Airport Road, and on her way to and from work, she noticed a car that fit the description of Bonnie's car parked alongside the road at Duval Road and Biscayne Boulevard. She called the police to report what she had noticed and hoped they would respond quickly. Maybe others had called in about seeing the other.

I was still pretty calm when I called my husband. He knew something was wrong by my voice. I explained that Bonnie was missing, that she and Mike argued, she left, and has not returned, with the police believing that Mike hurt her. I was confused about the television news release being aired without notifying the relatives first. She was not even missing for twelve hours yet. I did not know what to think or do at that point. Bob decided it would be best for him to come home for a week to find out what we should do. We did not understand how or why the police felt that there was foul play with Mike being a suspect so soon. He would be home Friday evening (the following evening).

At eight o'clock that night, who should come to the house? Not the police, but Mike's Aunt Annie. An aunt by marriage to Mike's uncle. The first words out of her mouth were, "I know he killed her. I just know Mike killed her." That is about all I remember her saying. I could not believe his aunt, whom he and Bonnie worked for, could say that. I really did not know Annie. I could not understand how she was so aware of what was going on in Bonnie and Mike's life and I knew nothing. I met Annie at Bonnie and Mike's wedding. Her only comment about the wedding was that it was a homemade wedding dress. Was that supposed to be a put-down? I did not feel they were wealthy.

I decided to call and tell the principal I would not be coming in tomorrow because of the situation. She understood and said I could take as much time off as needed. I was glad it was an understanding, Christian, private school.

Needless to say, I do not remember what we ate that night or how much sleep I got. That morning, Ginny did not want to go to school. She was intelligent and advanced beyond her grade level. I was glad I did not have to worry about her missing school. She was twelve at that time. Before I could think about anything, Annie was at the door. She said WE needed to pick Mike's son up at the daycare. The police would be at the daycare with papers. I did not know what this was about; however, I might finally find out from the police what they learned and why they had not contacted me. I was hoping for details that would shed some light on the situation. Good or bad.

The police were not there, and neither was Aaron. Annie seemed to know a lot about the daycare, even though Bonnie had never given her any legal right to pick Aaron up from the daycare. She learned people's names and the locations of Aaron's classroom and the administration office. Annie went to get Aaron. The administrator started to talk to me about allegations of sexual abuse when Annie came back in and said that Mike had abused Aaron. The administrator could not get another chance to speak. Bonnie had never mentioned that Aaron was abused or that Mike was abusing her, and yet Annie was saying that Mike abused them both! What next? Why did she know so much more than I did about what was happening to Bonnie and Aaron? I saw Bonnie at least weekly. I took care of Aaron often. I had Power of Attorney papers to care for Aaron. Surely Bonnie would have said something to me?

Annie was talking to someone on one of the first cell phones on the market. It sounded like a police officer on the way to the daycare, and when we left. Annie was adamant about finding Aaron and taking him to the CPT, whatever that was! So, our next stop was Aaron's home. No one was at their home. Annie's cell phone was dead. Since Annie had lived in Bonnie and Mike's home before they lived there, she knew the neighbor across the street. She asked this sweet older lady to use her phone. This lady had just lost her husband. I was so confused that I could not think of what to say to her as we stood outside waiting for Annie. Annie came out, and I was told WE were going to Mike's parents' house. The police would meet us there with the proper papers. I was not asked if I wanted to go or if I had any needs. I was in her vehicle, and I was going!

I just wanted to go home! This was not getting any easier, and I still did not know what was going on.

What or how am I supposed to act towards people whose son supposedly killed and abused my grandson and murdered my daughter? We arrived, and again, no police. We were let into Mike's parents' house. I could not believe Carol would even let us in. Carol led me to the rather dark den. I sat down on the nearest chair. I saw Aaron, his grandfather, and Mike on the opposite side of the room. John was holding Aaron, and Aaron was laughing at his grandfather. Then, Aaron would go to his dad to make him laugh. This went on for a short time. Aaron went back to John's daughter's room to play. They did not make me uncomfortable; however, I could not feel comfortable enough to talk or ask questions. I still felt like going home. The police arrived and spoke with Annie and Carol. The police did not have legal papers to take Aaron to CPT. They asked Mike if he would allow them to take Aaron to the CPT Center. Mike called his lawyer, and he said it should be okay if a relative went with Aaron. Aaron was three. what would it hurt for him to be interviewed? The officers said it should be a 45-minute interview.

I was ready to leave and walk home. It would have been a two-block walk. I should have followed my instincts. I just felt maybe I would find out some information and feel like I was the mother of the victim instead of a stranger just tagging along. Annie wanted me to sit in the back with Aaron. I felt too upset and did not want Aaron to be any more anxious than he must already be feeling. Aaron was comfortable and happy with his other grandma sitting by him. I ignored Annie and sat in the front seat.

As soon as we walked into the CPT "Child Protection Team" building, I saw the police officers and realized this was serious and happening. I did not consider it a significant concern without confirmation from the police. I put my hand over my mouth to stop from screaming and crying in front of Aaron. They all left the interim and closed the door, except for two officers. I lost it and sank to the floor. The officers said I needed to calm down, go to the bathroom, and straighten up, because they might need me to accompany Aaron into the interview room. I couldn't believe they would ask me to do that without prior warning or any consultation whatsoever.

We arrived at around ten o'clock. It took me time to pull myself together. I thought maybe the 45 minutes had passed, and I would not have to go into the interview room. Wrong again…I was taken to the interview room with Aaron. I was very nervous; however, Aaron helped me feel calm. He wanted me to hold him. Bree, the interviewer, was very unprofessional to me. I thought maybe she had already built a rapport with Aaron. It was evident that she did not. Whenever she asked a question about Aaron's mom, he would whine and cry. This went on for what seemed like hours. I interjected her line of questioning by asking Aaron everyday questions like What is your favorite color? What is your favorite animal at the zoo? Questions meant to distract his attention to pleasantries and things to calm him. Bree took the hint. When she came back to questioning about his mom, he would again whimper and cry.

I did not know what time it was or when or what Aaron had eaten, but I was hungry and tired. We were not given snacks or water. I felt the interview should be over. I started asking Aaron what his favorite food was and where he liked to eat to provide them with a hint. It was finally realized that yes, he might be hungry. It took another hour for the food to arrive. I do not understand why they did not just end the interview. We are talking about a three-year-old who did not know why he had not seen his mother, and did not understand what he was doing in that place. Aaron would not get down off my lap until Bree brought in the McDonald's Happy Meal, and she had left the room. He sat down at the little picnic table and ate his food. After he was finished, I suggested we play with the toys on the floor. We were playing with the toys for a while when Bree came in. I thought to say goodbye. No such luck!

I should have gotten up and said that the interview was over. Bree just came in and sat down in a way that put her in my space to play with Aaron. He was calm and in a playful mood. It would have been the time of day when he woke up from nap time, and it was time to play. The questions Bree asked I did not feel he was talking about events that happened recently or stories that were abusive in any way to anyone. It was playtime. When I thought that I could leave, and at least get something to drink. I motioned to Bree for me to leave the room—the officer who was monitoring opened the door and waved me out. The officer hugged me, said a few kind words, and led me to another door. During the brief time I was with the officer, I noticed a camera with a red light, indicating it was recording.

A short time later, we were asked to meet in the meeting room. It was around 2:30 at that time. I believe they did ask me if I wanted water. I was past wanting anything but to go home! Things just seemed to go from unbelievable to incredibly unbelievable. We waited for some time. The CPT investigator arrived, provided us with his card, and spoke with us. I am not sure what was said, except that it might be in Aaron's best interest to stay at our oldest daughter's home for now. At that point, I felt that might be best. Her home would be away from the drama that was taking place. We did not get back home until seven or eight o'clock. It had been a long day of no progress forward but progress backward.

Chapter Two:
The Start of Lies

Always tell the truth. That way, you don't have to remember what you said."

Mark Twain

Bob was home. We did not know more about what happened or transpired on days one and two. Bob went on a search to find Bonnie and gather information on Saturday. Our children started to arrive home to help us in any way they could.

On Sunday evening, around 8:00, the police finally came to talk to us. They wanted the names and addresses of relatives or places where Bonnie might have gone. They could not or would not answer our questions. We asked if Bonnie's car keys were in her purse. They refused to answer. We told them we knew of no reason Mike would harm Bonnie. For the most part, Bonnie and Mike seemed happy and always helped each other.

The officers told us that Bonnie's car had been found on Thursday night. The officers advised us not to talk to Mike or his parents. We were no better off than we were before they spoke to us. We could not understand that. It was alright to send me to John and Carol's house to pick Aaron up without a word from them about what was happening and berate me for breaking down and crying at the CPT, but now we were not to talk to them. Mike and his parents obviously knew what was and what was not in Bonnie's purse, so what was wrong with them telling us?

On a Sunday evening, in the rain and cold, Bob and I decided to go for a drive to think and try to make sense of what was happening. We even considered places where Mike might have hidden Bonnie alive and hurt. We still could not believe Mike would kill or harm Bonnie. We could not figure out what to do next or what to think.

Monday, Bob handed out posters that Annie had printed. I stayed home to manage the phone and well-wishers who came by to show their love and respect, and to see what services they could offer. I was unsure of what to do and could not offer any suggestions. I was in limbo. Bob and I still thought Bonnie could come home.

That was a day with no progress, too. On Tuesday, Bob accompanied the police search for Bonnie and/or clues. Bob was inclined to believe Bennie, Annie's husband and Mike's uncle, was leading the search. By Wednesday, we had decided that the only way to find out anything was to talk to Mike and his parents. We called them up and they said they would be right over. I was so glad we did. It was the first time that the situation became a way to move forward. Mike and his dad worked with Bob to gain information about Bonnie's depressive state of mind, what was in Bonnie's purse, and why the police thought Mike had hurt Bonnie.

Through Mike and his dad, we found out that when we were at the CPT, the police were searching Bonnie and Mike's house. They did not have a warrant. Mike permitted them to search. When Aaron said that Daddy ran over Mom with the truck, the truck was taken to the crime lab. When Aaron said something about Daddy hiding Mom, the house was searched for a body that could be hidden. I feel they were playing hide and seek, and Daddy found Mommy beside the bed. That was the point I decided to leave the interview room. I felt Aaron was playing, making up things that were playtime with Mom and Dad. The interview room was being recorded, so there's no need to worry, right?

We found out from Mike and his dad that Bonnie went with Annie on January 2, 1993. Bonnie had put down a deposit for an apartment in Orange Park that she was separating from her husband. The next day, she and Aaron picked up the deposit on the way to see her grandma in Palatka. That does not seem as though she was serious. Bonnie told me she wanted Aaron to stay away from Orange

Park. Why would she be looking for an apartment in Orange Park? Could it be that that is what Annie wanted Bonnie to do?

One apartment manager advised Bob to obtain a credit report, which they did, and it provided helpful information. The lead detective said they needed a grand jury subpoena to do that. Why was the apartment manager able to do a credit check so fast? Didn't the police have more authority than an apartment manager? The apartment manager that Bonnie left a deposit with said that Aaron liked the apartment and that Bonnie seemed serious about the apartment when Aaron was not even with her that day, only on the day she picked up the deposit.

We found out that Annie was at the daycare twice on January 7, 1993. The first time she was denied access to take Aaron because she had no legal forms and was not on the parents' list who could pick Aaron up from the daycare. Bennie then called the police to go to the daycare to speak to Aaron. Bennie asked questions directed at the daycare staff as Annie went to find Aaron. The teacher tried to hear what Annie was saying to Aaron. Annie pulled Aaron out of the room for about fifteen to twenty minutes. Annie said it was only a minute or two. When Aaron came back to class, he had a blank stare, like he had been scared. Aaron was not receptive to the teachers and was very upset the rest of the day. The next day, Aaron did not want to go to the daycare. He did not want to be alone with Annie at the CPT center either. The staff member in the daycare office, questioned by Annie and Bennie, asked who the police officer was. She thought the person questioning was a police officer. That was not the case. The police officer asked no questions. The officer was not able to take Aaron from the daycare because he had no legal papers; however, they did call the child abuse hotline since Bonnie felt Aaron might have been abused. Evidently, Bonnie felt that Aaron was abused sometime in the first part of November.

Bonnie talked to the staff at the daycare. Bonnie indicated that a man may have abused Aaron. The daycare staff reassured Bonnie that no one at the daycare had an opportunity to abuse Aaron. Bonnie said that only two men could have been responsible for something to Aaron. One was Mike, and the other was Trey, Annie and Bennie's son, who was around 21 years old at that time.

On January 25, 1993, Aaron had another interview with CPT. Aaron did not say anything against anyone. HRS, now called Children and Family Services, which found the allegations of abuse unfounded, gave Aaron back to Mike. After the first CPT interview, the CPT investigator who was there at the first interview with Aaron and talked to us reported that allegations of abuse were unfounded. HRS said they were unfounded on both the first CPT interview and the second. Annie was outraged by those findings! It was clear that Annie had tainted the evidence of Aaron's interview because she had talked to Aaron the day before and frightened him, according to the daycare staff.

Somehow, the video from the first CPT interview was no longer in existence, and Aaron supposedly stated that Daddy shot Mommy. This happened after I left the interview room. I was given a transcript of the interview that Bree wrote two weeks after the interview. I was to make changes in the margins on the manuscript. I made many! The officer viewing the interview's notes was also different from Bree's. No guns were taken from Mike at the time of the first interview. When Aaron mentioned that Daddy ran Mommy over with the truck, Mike's work truck was taken to the police lab. When Aaron mentioned something about Daddy and hiding Mommy, the Police looked for hiding places. Also, the CPT investigator who was present at the interview stated that allegations of abuse were unfounded. HRS also noted that the claims of abuse were unfounded. If Aaron said Daddy shot Mommy, wouldn't the police have taken Mike's guns? Wouldn't the investigator and HRS say that that was cause to believe Aaron was abused by being present at a violent scene of his mother being shot by his father? Aaron did not look or indicate in any way that he was traumatized or scared, recalling a violent memory. There is something amiss with this shift in the events, warranting further investigation into what Aaron supposedly stated. Were the HRS and the CPT authorities asked why they felt the allegations were unfounded? Not that we could ever find. No depositions seem to confirm how these two professionals could conclude that the claims of abuse were unfounded.

During January, several people who contacted the police or were interviewed by the police during their investigation identified seeing Bonnie on January 7, 1993, the day after Bonnie went missing. One woman, whose relatives knew me from the school where I worked, was adamant that her relative knew something about Bonnie's disappearance. If Bonnie was alive on January 7, 1993, Mike could not have harmed her on January 6 or even in the wee morning hours of January 7. Aaron could not have witnessed his dad hurting his mom either.

There was a maintenance man and a head maid who stated that a man showed a great deal of interest in the dumpster the morning the purse was found. The man's observation began on the balcony of the second floor and then proceeded to within a few feet of the dumpster, where Bonnie's purse was found, until the police arrived. This man was identified and located in South Florida later in January, was brought to the police station for another crime of stalking, and told our police that they needed to question him. The lead homicide detective stated to their police that we have our man. Our police reported that they questioned him, and the man did not have any information about Bonnie. No police report was found of what they asked him, why he was so interested in the dumpster, or if he saw who put the purse in the dumpster.

There were people in different establishments on Airport Road who identified Bonnie with another man and/or a woman, all of whom were on Airport Road. There were even two different, unrelated people who identified Bonnie with a man at a restaurant the day before eating lunch together. These individuals were all reported as unreliable witnesses for various reasons. How could they all be unreliable about seeing Bonnie on the same day and in the same area where she was seen on January 7? Yet, believe two individuals who had a questionable past and relationship with my daughter in the last six months she lived in this area.

Annie was able to convince GAL (Guardian Ad Litem) that Mike abused Aaron in some way, shape, or form to become involved in the case. GAL, along with CPT are extension of the police department. They do not seem to be impartial in finding facts and information about the case. Their desires seem to fit Annie's! HRS deemed to drop the case on February 8, 1993. They did not want to be a party in this case.

Annie talking to Aaron and Aaron's reluctance to be alone with Annie the next day seem to indicate that she tainted anything Aaron might understand about knowledge of his mother's whereabouts. Bree's shredding of her notes, combined with the lack of video or audio recordings of the interview, renders her statement hearsay. Aaron has even testified several times that he could not and cannot remember anything about January 6, 1993

We asked the police on several occasions what real evidence they had that Mike killed Bonnie. They had no crime scene, no body, and no confirmed motive for Mike wanting to harm Bonnie. They could never answer those questions, and yet they never changed their desire to hold Mike as the one who committed foul play on Bonnie. They did not investigate a live Bonnie. They stated that a relative said that Mike murdered Bonnie. Annie is not a relative of Bonnie, which is a misconception. No evidence of why Mike might kill Bonnie or a body, or even a crime scene. That was good enough for us to look for real facts, but it was good enough for the police to put all their efforts into the murder of Bonnie. The relatives were by marriage an aunt and uncle. That does not make them close enough to parents and siblings. The police did not check with Bonnie's parents or even the records of these relatives. Many people they talked to said they should check out this aunt and uncle.

Even though Annie's allegations that Bonnie was planning to leave Mike and move into an apartment in Orange Park did not pan out, Annie and Bennie said that Bonnie was having an affair with Kurt G., who worked for them. They said that it happened in November 1992. This became the motive for Mike's foul play.

We were able to receive the police report where Annie and Bennie made that statement about Bonnie having an affair with Kurt G. to them. The police brought Kurt G. to the police station for questioning. Much of the report was blacked out. However, he supposedly stated that Bonnie called him after Thanksgiving break to tell him she missed him and wanted to be with him. This leads him to become emotionally attached to Bonnie. Kurt and Bonnie first kissed in mid-December. Bonnie then bought two football tickets for a big football game on New Year's Eve. She and Kurt, while Mike was at the game, went to the Sunshine Inn for about an hour. Bonnie told Kurt she was moving into an apartment about a week before she disappeared. Kurt said they decided to continue the relationship without commitments. Another part was blacked out. Kurt was then asked if he knew what happened to Bonnie. He said he didn't and would take a polygraph.

The polygraph submitted was not that of Kurt G. but of Curt J.

Annie made another statement, claiming that Bonnie's best friend at work had told her about an affair Bonnie was having with Curt J. This took place at a breakfast at the end of December. Why did Annie and Bennie say it was Kurt G.? Annie usually didn't come to work early enough to go out for breakfast. Annie's story keeps getting more unbelievable.

Another detective reported that Bonnie's best friend from High School, who was the last person to see Bonnie the night she disappeared, told the officer that Bonnie had an affair with Curt J. This best friend found out at the end of December. With conflicting stories, you would think the police would try to find the TRUTH. How could Kurt G. and Curt J.'s statements be so similar and yet not confirmed by facts? No deposition of the friends and no records of the Sunshine Inn.

The police could have confirmed the whole affair by visiting the Sunshine Inn and checking who checked in between 7:00 and 8:00 on December 31, 1992, and with whom. Kurt G. stated that he checked in with his name. Curt J. made the same statement at the trial in 2019. Too bad

Mike's lawyer did not find out if it happened, and if it did, with whom.

Seeing the two K/Curts made me very suspicious. I began to wonder if Kurt had read a paper and was supposed to sign it, stating that what he read was fact. After reading it, he said no, he had never had an affair with Bonnie, and he would not sign it! He would take a polygraph. Kurt's employment with Annie and Bennie was removed from the company records; however, when I searched the internet, I found that Kurt did work for Annie and Bennie at that time. I could not get my computer to print it out. It gave his address, too. If I could get that information, I did not know why Mike's lawyer could not find Kurt G.! I made sure Mike's lawyers had the information. His lawyers did not even depose Kurt G. or Bonnie's friends.?

Bob and I were giving the police information that we received about the case; however, they were not reciprocating. Still not answering our first questions about Bonnie's car keys or what the pills found in her purse and at her home were. Instead, we were not cooperating, and we had lied to them. They never said when or what those lies were. We stated that they had lied about the credit report, police obtaining mail from her place of work (they said they could not legally do that), and obtaining a license plate owner. They said that the license plate was not issued. We found out the county and the city where the plates were issued. We were not able to find the person or business. Yet we were the ones not cooperating and lying.

Through our investigation, we found out that Annie has always been a controlling type of person, from people who went to school with her and family members. At every junction, she has controlled this case. Bonnie never wanted to go to work for Annie and Bennie. Bonnie gave in after a year or so after she and Mike married. She did not want to buy Annie and Bennie's old house. She and Mike went ahead and bought the house. Bonnie and Mike tried to be good workers for them. It must have worn thin in 1992. There seemed to be a switch in Bonnie's overall feelings about Mike's parents and our family. She seemed to push Mike's parents out and us more into their lives. Mike came to me in May of 1992 to ask why she avoided his parents and why Bonnie was unhappy. He also stated that he noticed some passing of pills around the office at work. I mentioned that wouldn't Annie have stopped that from happening? He did not know or would not say if Annie knew. He asked if I could find out why Bonnie was so sad about life and distant from his parents.

Bonnie came over on Mother's Day while Mike was visiting his mother's house, not together as they normally did. At one point, I asked Bonnie about her life. She did not have much to say. I asked why the distance between her and her in-laws. I reminded her how close they used to be. She just kind of shrugged it off, saying I just didn't know or understand. I told her I knew what it was like to have in-laws who were not supportive of their son's marriage to a poor farm girl. She ended by restating that I just didn't know or understand, with no elaboration. I then asked about pills being passed around at work. I reminded her how dangerous that was to your mind and body. I stated that her attitude might change if she stopped taking the pills. She did not seem upset but left soon afterward.

I saw Bonnie happier and doing crafty-type things like sewing for Aaron and herself. She and Mike changed the extra bedroom into a family room with a workout space for Mike, a sewing space for Bonnie and Aaron's video space. For Aaron's birthday on August 29, 1992, she invited Mike's whole family and was assured Mike's whole family would all be there at Aaron's birthday party. I thought that was great and showed a definite change in Bonnie. Annie and Bennie came a little late. I guess it was a fashionable late for them. The first thing Bennie said was, "If they are staying (looking and pointing to Mike's whole family including Bennie's mother), then we are leaving." Bonnie said, "They are staying!" Annie and Bennie put Aaron's gifts down and left. No one was upset and the party went on. That was a big indication that Bonnie was not concerned about what Annie wanted. Bonnie seemed ready to control her life and listen to her own needs. Does that seem like something that Annie was likely to condone!?

About a month later, Bonnie called to see if I could take care of Aaron for the day so she could go job hunting. I said I would. She brought Aaron over in the morning. She was dressed nicely. Right around 10:30, Bonnie called to ask if all was okay. She told me that if work called, not to let them know she was looking for another job. I asked, "What if Mike called?" She laughed and said that was okay. He had helped her write her resume the night before. When she came to pick Aaron up, she seemed happy. Annie thought she was having a mole removed on the back of her neck. If Annie asked about it, she would put a Band-Aid over it. It was more proof that Bonnie had had enough of Annie, and by Mike helping her write her resume, he was supporting her in finding a new job.

About a month later, Bonnie called almost hysterical, saying she wished she had taken the job at the radio station down the road. She wanted a job as a bookkeeper at Memorial Hospital and waited to hear from them. The one at the radio station seemed more like a dead-end job to her. She did not say why she had become so upset with not finding work elsewhere. This was an indication of just how serious she was about leaving her present job with Annie and Bennie. It seemed apparent that her attitude about her employers had not changed in the past month or two.

In late October, Bonnie and Mike began setting up a new office in Gainesville for Annie and Bennie. I thought everything must have settled down. Maybe Mike and Bonnie would eventually move to Gainesville to solve family problems. I hated to see them move, but it might be better for them. In the middle of November, I cared for Aaron while Mike and Bonnie went to San Francisco with Annie and Bennie for a tool convention. Bonnie had Power of Attorney papers drawn up for me to care for Aaron. That was a little discomforting to me. She never did that before! I found out later that she had written a will and had them both notarized by Annie on the same day, November 5, 1992. The Power of Attorney and the Will said the same thing, giving me custody of Aaron if, for any reason, Mike could not care for Aaron.

When they came home and picked Aaron up, they seemed really happy and a little giddy. I asked what was up. They sat very close and seemed like teenagers. They said Annie and Bennie tried to keep them separated the whole trip. They outsmarted them and went off on their own excursions. They were very happy. This is when Bonnie was supposed to be thinking about leaving Mike and having an affair. Does that sound likely to you? When did she even have time to think about that when she was running to Gainesville many times during the week to set up an office, getting ready for Thanksgiving and Christmas, and doing her other household duties? Having an affair with someone with whom both she and Mike worked. Bonnie was far from stupid, as that seemed to be. Curt J. had just married, and

Bonnie was supposed to be the real person to initiate the affair. Does not seem to be the Bonnie I knew.

Mike must have had a hard time trying to keep up with her. Being that he was possessive and had to know where she was at all times! I am not sure what I saw between them during this time, whether it was Mike being possessive or abusive. He did seem protective. He seemed overprotective by calling to make sure she was alright. I could not understand the need. I could not see that as possessive or abusive. Bonnie did not seem upset over it. What was the need to make sure she was where she said she was going to be?

Right after Christmas, Mike said Bonnie was quiet and unhappy again. She would not tell him why or what he had done. It was to the point where he asked her if she wanted a divorce. He said he would move out. Bonnie said she would move out. He tried to convince her it would be better if he moved out. He asked me to talk to her. I said I thought things were better. He said he thought they were, too, for a while. I was confused, but of course I would do my best to talk to her.

Bonnie asked me to take care of Aaron in early January 1993 while she and Mike went to the funeral of their next-door neighbor. I thought I would have a chance to talk to Bonnie again about being sad. That did not happen. She seemed to avoid talking to me about her unhappiness with life with Mike and Aaron. I would keep on trying. There was no urgent reason, or was there?

Chapter Three:
Trying to Find the Truth

"Justice consists not in being neutral between right and wrong, but finding out the right and upholding it where it is found, against the wrong."

Theodore Roosevelt

In February 1993, Bob and I were not only trying to find out what happened to Bonnie but also trying to get Aaron reunited with his dad, or at least give his dad visitation rights as well as visitation rights for us. How could this be happening to this family? Why were we being torn apart? How could we believe Mike was innocent and that made us party to be on opposite sides of the police? Just give us evidence to believe a crime was committed!

I went back to work. This was costing money. Bob quit his job and requested his 401 (k) money so we could still find out what happened to Bonnie and pay for life expenditures. That would get us through a year. We used Mike's family lawyer for Aaron's reunification and visitation rights for a while, paying for our portion of her work. After a few months, it became evident that we needed our own lawyer. We also hired a private investigator. The police did not seem to be helping us, and we could not trust their information or their willingness to give us any new information.

Bob and I wrote many letters to agencies that might help or provide information, to government agencies, and to different politicians at various levels. They all wished us well but said they could not help us. It seems it was not in their job description or to that effect. They would not confirm or deny what the police told them. Bob went directly to some government agencies that were THERE TO HELP GOOD CITIZENS. We had some who gave us some information, then said later Oops, I shouldn't have given that to you. One such time, they saw a report about Bonnie on a desk in the federal courthouse. Bob and I suspected Bonnie was in the Witness Protection Program.

Annie and Bennie had a bad habit of creating their own IRS bookkeeping records. Since Annie was listed as the owner of the business. The IRS did not want to deal with a jury that felt sorry for a female business owner. The IRS gave her a slap on the hand with a fine and penalties. Bennie's first partner in another tool business relinquished the partnership because of Bennie's unethical business practices. Bennie was accused of threatening the life of the partner's family if he carried the matter any further. The partner did not take it any further.

We had information that Bonnie's secret bank account was SECRET even to Bonnie! Her friend at work told police that she heard Bonnie yelling and screaming at Annie and Bennie about account records that she knew nothing about. Bonnie was supposed to be the business bookkeeper. Bonnie came out of their office crying. We thought this information was enough evidence that indicated Bonnie might know more about Annie and Bennie's business than they liked anyone to know about. Might be enough information to investigate Annie and Bennie. Bonnie's friend no longer worked for Annie and Bennie. No deposition or report on this incident.

I wrote a letter to Bonnie and gave it to the office in the criminal department section at the federal courthouse to see if Bonnie could be in the witness protection program. Of course, we did not have any information to deliver the letter, such as a changed name or identification number. That strategy worked against us. We did not want Annie or Bennie to know that she may be in the witness protection program.

That letter I wrote to Bonnie was brought up at a court hearing. The judge said Bonnie was not in the witness protection program. We were made out to be distraught parents or a little crazy, maybe. Perhaps that made us unfit to be Aaron's guardians. Maybe it was to tell Annie and Bennie she was not out to get them. We talked to other people who had connections with federal law enforcement, who said their sources could not find her in the program. We had two contacts who said there was a chance she could be deep into the system. One contact said this is where she could be and where to track her for a few years. One of the first locations was close to us. A small town in the small town of Switzerland. A small town just south of us that did not want me to post a sign about her disappearance.

There were custody hearings that we were allowed to go to. For some hearings, we were not allowed to or were not invited to go into. Some court room sessions our oldest daughter was allowed to go to and we were not. There seemed to be three people who could go to any of the hearings they chose. Those three people were Annie, Bennie, and Lamar, their lawyer.

When we were not there, they would lie or make accusations that they did not have any evidence to validate the truth of the allegations they made. One item was that Bonnie told our oldest daughter that Bonnie thought her dad might have abused her. We did not have any chance to defend this accusation. Bob had a top security clearance. He was in the military while Bonnie grew up. He was on active duty. We had five girls and one boy. Does this sound plausible that he could have sexually abused one daughter? Our children did not have rooms of their own. I would wake up during the night for one of the younger children to see or hear anything unusual going on in our home. Anne and Bennie seem to stop at nothing to belittle Bob and me. They seemed to put wedges between us and our children. We had no way to prove what we did or did not do in our home or defend our parenthood.

We asked the police again what the pills were that were found in Bonnie's purse and her home. We were told they were not analyzed yet. We never could find out what they were other than red, white, and blue in a police report. This was another time too late that we wished we could go back and have saved a pill bottle for ourselves to be analyzed. That is all police reports ever stated red, white, and blue. What type of analysis is that? The lead detective said they were unimportant. To us they were. If she kept the pills that were given to her in the office and Annie knew about the sharing or was even party to it, it would explain Bonnie's change of attitude during her last year of working at that company. It would indicate another point in the way business was run at Annie and Bennie's. What else were Annie and Bennie into?

We asked about Bonnie's car key. We were not able to receive an answer to that. EVER! If Mike did see or have them, then why was it a secret? That never made any sense other than to cover a police maneuver, keeping us and others from knowing that whoever drove the car into the long-term parking area still had the car key. So, who drove the car into the parking lot?

We inquired about the records of the long-term parking area. We were given one excuse after another why they couldn't get a report. We were told they did not show who drove the car to the area where it was found. We now have the report that was given to the police. The report covered the period from January 6, 1993, at 10:30 pm to January 7, 1993, at 2:00 pm. If they had asked for the report for the time ending at 5:00 or 6:00 p.m. on January 7, they would have had the time that Bonnie's car pulled into the long-term parking area. Just a few hours after the vehicle was found. Another one of those OOPs we don't know. Bad for you. Good for us. Why do I feel sick when I look back and see the mistakes they made? Is it stupidity, ineptness, or someone's arrogance to have things go their way?

Also on February 22, 1993, in the psychologist's therapy room, Aaron stated, "Mommy and Daddy in the yard." Then Aaron became hysterical, then said "sink in the lake..Mommy sink in lake her car too." Aaron calls Mom Bonnie.

This might have been important if there could have been some truth to what he said. However, Bonnie's car was not, nor has it ever been, in a lake. Bonnie's body was never found in a lake. Aaron supposedly showed him where that body of water may have been. I never knew Aaron to call his mom Bonnie.

It sounds as if Aaron is repeating something that he heard, rather than an event that happened in his life. Adults sometimes talk, thinking children are out of hearing range, about what they are saying, but the children are listening. These children may take things out of context or not put what they hear, only part of the story, that does not relate to them.

In April of 1992, many people involved in the disappearance of Bonnie were told by police not to talk to us or our private investigator. This made gathering information more difficult, but we persevered. We had friends who were also helping in different capacities to gain information.

During a deposition, Bob and I were questioned by the CPT lawyer. Most of the questions concerned whether Bonnie had any problems with her car or if she had been in an accident. Another question was why we were searching in certain areas, and why we suspected Annie and Bennie were involved. They did not seem to be interested in what or how we felt about Bonnie's disappearance, or information that would help Aaron. Why wasn't Aaron their primary concern? Where were their questions about Bonnie and Aaron's relationship? Or how Mike treated Aaron?

Bob talked to the CPT investigator on the January eighth CPT interview on April 9, 1993, who again said he reported that there was no basis for abuse, and it was classified as unfounded. This investigator appears to have been removed as the investigator after the CPT's first interview. The new investigator found that there was cause to be concerned that abuse may have been committed. Still not an affirmative cause to panic or a cause for Aaron to be uprooted from all immediate family members.

Mike's lawyer's partner was at the federal courthouse on April 9, 1993. She said she saw a girl who looked like Bonnie get into a white sedan with a male driver with Florida tag number EVE 94 D. Our PI ran the plate, and it came back not found. Bob looked at license plates to see if he could find any EVE plates. He was unsuccessful. The lead homicide detective said no such License plate was issued. How could a lawyer identify a license number as wrong? We did finally find out the county and city, but not the person for the EVE portion of the tag. The homicide detective said Bob misunderstood that it was the part he could not find.

Aaron seems to be talking about a monster sticking his finger up his butt. Aaron mentioned different men who did this. One time, he mentioned his dad. For sure, CPT was sure it must have been his dad. A doctor was ordered to find out. The doctor said there was no evidence to confirm or deny the allegation. There was no evidence to suggest that Mike even had the opportunity to commit the act. Would he even have done anything when so many people were waiting for some indiscretion? Of course, there were court hearings to take away all visitation rights from all relatives except for our oldest daughter, her husband, and children.

During April and May, we continued writing letters and searching for individuals who might have information about Bonnie. Some would not get involved. Police told some not to talk to us or our PI. One was a friend's daughter who worked at a Little Champ close to Airport Road. She may have seen Bonnie on January 7, 1993. We were not able to confirm that. Another was the relative of parents from the school where I worked. Bob and I went to her house after I called, leaving a message on her phone that we would see her the next morning at 9:00. When we arrived, the police were already there. An officer came to our car and told us Gail did not want to talk to us or our PI.

I couldn't believe that the police were already there before us. It just confirmed what we thought. Our phone was bugged. I decided to write a letter to Gail. Our PI went to her workplace and was finally willing to talk to our PI. She called the police on January 8, 1993, and reported that she had seen Bonnie the previous afternoon, January 7, 1993. The police told her she could not have seen Bonnie. Why couldn't she have seen Bonnie? She did see Bonnie at around 4:00 in the car described on the news in the long-term airport parking lot. She said Bonnie was standing outside the vehicle with an older woman. Gail worked for Budget Rent-A-Car. When she drove by twenty minutes later, Bonnie and the woman were gone, but the car's emergency lights were flashing.

Annie, Bennie, and the lead homicide detective were getting a little nervous. We were receiving information through various sources that we were not supposed to receive. The police were pressuring our PI to stop his investigation into Bonnie's disappearance. They went so far as to raid his car dealership and tell them to stop, or the police would file charges against his business. He would lose his company, which he needed. We had to find another PI.

Chapter Four:
What Gives What Takes

"Integrity is telling the truth. That way, you don't have to remember what you said."

Mark Twain

Mike's work truck was given back to Bennie. Other items were never taken, like other vehicles, except Bonnie's. The guns were not taken, then taken two weeks later. The guns were tested and fired, and shells were put in the police storage with other items classified as evidence two weeks later. All the police notes were typed. A copy was given to the officer, and another was placed in the archives, which the police were unable to locate for the 2019 trial. We could not find the video. It seemed to have been moved from one location to another, and we were told that there was no video. It seems Brees' notes were shredded after the interview. I suppose that is why the minutes of what Aaron said and what happened during the five or six hours he was at the CPT center did not align with the detective's notes and my notes after Bree rewrote her notes.

The police still could not produce any evidence that a crime had been committed. They would not drop the case or explain the reasons why Aaron was not with his father, except that Aaron stated that Mike had hurt Bonnie. That was changed to Daddy shot mommy. The only so-called evidence they had was a partial heel print that could be Mike's on the back floor of her car. If it were on a police show, it would be laughed at as evidence that a husband killed his wife. Where was the crime scene, the body, any relative evidence to show a crime had been committed?

Things were thrown out of the glove compartment of Bonnie's car. We heard (hearsay) that Bennie was the one who did that, looking for a radar detector that he supposedly bought for Bonnie. There was a receipt that Bonnie had bought a radar detector. Bennie's fingerprint was found in the glove compartment. It makes sense that Bonnie's purse was placed in a way that would be noticed in the dumpster, there were no prints elsewhere, and the car was positioned to be visible from the road with its flashers on. Does that seem like a person who would leave a mess in the glove compartment? The keys were not in the car, her purse, or the doors were unlocked. That indicates to me the person wanted the car discovered fast.

Bennie stated in an interview with police that Mike looked scared as hell on January 7, 1993. Who would not have that type of look who was trying to make sense of their missing spouse, whose personal belongings were found in a dumpster? I did not know what was going on. I tried not to feel or look scared in front of my students on that day. I do not know what I looked like, nor did I care what I looked like. Why would Mike?

There was no evidence of a crime against the husband, let alone his parents or the parents of the victim, and yet they were held guilty of an unknown crime or circumstance that warranted a separation from their grandchild or be held guilty of a wrongdoing forever. Does this really make sense? These same people have proven to be reliable parents in the eyes of professionals. Yet, they are supposedly guilty according to a few individuals who have or could have been proven unreliable. Anyone who expressed interest in stating that these "guilty" people were honest and good citizens was taken off the case.

Aaron's psychologist and caregivers stated that Aaron was upset after visitation with his dad and grandparents. It stands to reason that a child who is taken away from people that he loves would be upset after being taken away from them time and time again. That happens even when real, proven abuse takes place. A child wants stability with the ones they know and love.

People who might talk to Mike, Mike's dad, us, or our PI were told not to speak to us. What could these people tell us that would hurt their case against Mike? It could be that what they could say would indicate that Mike was a hard worker, a good husband, and a good father. Maybe Annie and Bennie should be investigated instead of Mike!?

So far, there had been no evidence of foul play or abuse of any kind, and no police reports against Mike from authorities, co-workers, or friends. The police could not even file charges. The only negative accounts were made by Annie and Bennie, who made conflicting statements. They could not even prove that an affair happened other than from a statement by a married man who worked for Annie and Bennie. Annie and Bennie stated that the affair was by another employee who would not collaborate with the statement that the event ever happened.

My husband was told that another police officer, who knew Bennie, called Bennie when he noticed the last name of the purse's owner. He called Bennie to see if he knew Bonnie. Bennie and Annie had time to think about what they would do with that knowledge. This officer was not mentioned in the police reports we obtained. This same officer made statements about Bennie's sexual harassment cases, that Bennie bragged about, and that Bennie was or once was a reserve police officer. This indicates a person who lacks respect for others. It was all about him. I thank God for the information we found or were given us by a reliable source. It all helped to make sense of the other information we received that the police had suppressed.

Chapter Five:
More Facts

"The truth may hurt for a little while, but a lie hurts forever."

Anonymous

We received information that a retired security guard saw Bonnie on January 7, 1993. The guard was good at her job and good at remembering faces. With the aid of a composite artist, she could make a composite drawing of the male she saw Bonnie with on that day.

The lead detective informed us that they do not have someone available to create a composite drawing. Bob asked several individuals connected to the media venue if they knew of someone who could do a composite drawing. The lead detective from Missing Persons provided us with the name of the sheriff's son who creates sketches for the city police department. Another "misunderstanding" of the lead homicide detective. It took several weeks to schedule an appointment for the sketch to be completed.

The police were very reluctant to give a copy to my husband, would not give it to the media, and did not show it to other witnesses to make it a viable sketch. Mike's attorney was able to provide us with one. We seem to be running in circles to get to a point that solidifies whether we are looking for a living Bonnie or not. Why were the police, especially the lead homicide detective, giving us such a difficult time?

We heard about another eyewitness who saw Bonnie on January 7, 1993. She is a friend's sister who worked at a convenience store off Airport Road. She had worked at a convenience store for several years. She was good at remembering faces. We do not have any added information. Evidently, she had been told not to talk to us or our PI. She was afraid of police reprisal for her husband and child's sake.

I had questions about the accuracy of police records typed up from the officer's notes. I thought they audio-taped the interviews and had the tape transcribed. There were several errors made in what I said, as well as in what Bob and other people interviewed said, which were not stated accurately. One that keeps popping up is that an officer asked me about Bonnie's car keys, and I gave them to him. I was never asked about Bonnie's car keys. I had never held Bonnie's car keys. This is important because it means Bonnie could have kept her car keys, or the person who last drove her car could have kept them. That would be an indication Bonnie was alive on January 7, 1993. Perhaps they should have left the car where it was parked to see if someone would come back to claim it.

Another interview that changed from the police interview was with Gail Billings, the woman who worked for Budget Rent-A-Car. The police report states that Gail believes she saw Bonnie and her aunt wearing sunglasses in a garage by the airport rental office. Our interview with the P.I. revealed that Gail saw Bonnie and an older woman at around 4:00 p.m. in the airport's long-term parking lot. Twenty minutes later, the women were gone, and the emergency flashers were flashing. Right where the police found her car with the emergency lights flashing. The police questioned her many times. Gail's story never changed. Again, if Bonnie were alive, Mike could not have killed her, and Aaron could not have witnessed Daddy killing her.

Bonnie's emergency flashers would explain all the questions about Bonnie having an accident or car problems. There were no accidents or car problems. The reason appears to be that Bonnie wanted the public to know she was alive and to focus on figuring out what the real problem was.

One exceptional deposition that Mike's lawyer gave to a state department employee was in March 1993. In the deposition, Erlene stated that she observed Aaron and Mike playing together. There was no fear or apprehension. Aaron had a good relationship with his dad.

When asked about her opinion of Annie, Erlene said she felt uneasy. There were some inconsistencies in what Annie told her. Annie said there was contention between my oldest daughter and Mike, but when she talked to our oldest daughter, there had been no contention, bad feelings, or bickering. She told Erlene that Annie and Bennie were paying for the daughter's attorney to care for Aaron. The daughter was advised not to disclose information to Annie and Bennie or allow them to have contact with Aaron. It seemed to be a consistent feeling among many people that Annie and Bennie were not completely truthful in their statements.

Annie said that Aaron was afraid of Mike and that he shied away from Mike. That is not what Erlene observed when she monitored Mike and Aaron at visitation. She said there was a good bond between Aaron and Mike. No one else could see any damaging relationship between Aaron and his dad.

When Mike regained custody of Aaron on February 5, 1993, Annie called Erlene to stop that action. Erlene could not stop it. Annie went to great lengths to prevent Mike from obtaining custody, and she did receive that stoppage. Aaron was taken from Mike. Mike received visitation rights, nothing more. Annie tried very hard to relinquish that right and was able to do that, too.

Other people who found Annie questionable were at Aaron's daycare. In the deposition, Erlene spoke to Aaron's daycare workers. Annie put words in their mouths. Annie would say that Bonnie told her Mike was abusive and abused Aaron. That is not what the daycare workers told Erlene. If

Bonnie said things to that effect, the daycare would have reported it to the abuse hotline. What the daycare told Erlene was that in the first part of December 1993, Bonnie was concerned about Aaron. He was having nightmares and did not want to go to the bathroom, and when he did, it hurt. She asked the daycare workers to speak with him to see if Aaron would talk to them. Aaron did talk to his teacher. The outcome was that he was afraid of the monster. When Aaron said the monster was Mister and that Mister was daddy, she stopped questioning him. Kay told Bonnie she should take him to a doctor. Bonnie stated that the only two men who were around Aaron were his dad, Mike, and Trey, Annie, and Bennie's son. Bonnie told her the doctor said pinworms could cause those problems. Erlene talked to friends and neighbors who stated they saw no violence or abuse. Bonnie and Mike were good people who were helpful to one another and others. The neighbors did not hear or see any disturbance on the night of January 6 or at any other time.

Visitations were difficult. We were all happy to see Aaron, but it was rough to say goodbye. We never knew what the advisers would say about the visits. We had to have them videotaped to ensure that lies would not hold up as grounds for ending visits. Of course, allegations were made about Aaron's bad behavior after the visits. Anything to make life unbearable except for the adversary or those who wanted Aaron taken away from Mike and his grandparents. I am so thankful for my beliefs. The peace and comfort come from the truth of the circumstances of this nightmare. They found the videotapes damaging their case and had the judge stop Mike's family from videotaping the visitations.

Mike was able to incorporate the assistance of another psychologist to interview with Aaron. The psychologist was well-known. He stated that he saw Aaron with no post-traumatic stress syndrome. Dr. Kropp said Aaron was well-adjusted, especially for what he has experienced, not living with his mom or dad. Dr. Kropp stated that Aaron was suffering from attachment syndrome and should be with his dad. Even this did not sway the court from doing anything different from the desires of Annie or Bennie.

Annie and Bennie were now trying to press charges against Mike and his father for entering Annie and Bennie's condo in St. Augustine. It seems not to have gone too far. I now wonder why that was strange. Looking back, I wonder why that was not listed as property Annie and Bennie owned. They supposedly owned a business in St. Augustine and the property in Gainesville, where Bonnie and Mike were preparing for the new business operation. Of course, at some point, the business in St. Augustine folded. It seems to be some phony business practice. This has been especially true for me since, in 2018, the business in Gainesville was rated as a five-star business, but its office was located in a run-down strip mall with very little parking. Adjacent to this business was a used car lot that curved around to the backside of the building. There is no real business for loading and unloading supplies. This did not appear to be an operating business!?

In August of 1993, we were allowed to take Aaron to Disney World. It was a good time for us and our youngest daughter. Our oldest daughter and her two children were going on the same days. GAL wanted our itinerary. Who makes an itinerary when they go to a theme park? What would be so bad about meeting Katie and Kyle there? I guess it wasn't considered proper for us to take one grandchild without inviting all of our grandchildren. They all had mothers and fathers. Aaron had neither.

Aaron was not able to see us, his dad, or his other grandparents for his fourth birthday. Why was it so necessary to do this to a child?

Bob talked to Bonnie's best friend from high school in September. Sandy seemed to be saying what Annie told her to say. Sandy mentioned dates and happenings similar to Annie's. However, Annie told the police that Bonnie's best friend at work told her about the affair. That means two people knew about the affair before Annie. That means Annie was not as close to Bonnie as she made herself out to be! Neither of these best friends played an essential role in this case. It is hearsay as to what her best friends knew about the disappearance of Bonnie or Bonnie's feelings toward Mike, or if she had an affair. The police cannot prove that she and Kurt, or Curt, were at the Sunshine Inn in December. We do not know if Bonnie gave Sandy money, or how much, or if she did. My husband said it was because Sandy is blonde! She is a sweet girl who once worked for Annie and Bennie.

Aaron started talking about a monster sticking his finger up his butt again. Why did this start up again? This was happening in February 1993. This went on through June—no audio or video tapes. I could believe it. However, the real question is, why did the finger in the butt start up again? Perhaps it is the separation from his mom and dad. Maybe he cannot distinguish between what is real and what is make-believe. Leading questions asked by someone about who the monster might be or what the monster did might be to answer questions that had no real meaning to his real-life happenings. Whoever the monster was in December 1992 is not remembered, but the event is. Dr. Kropp did not see any negative facts concerning Aaron and Mike during his sessions with Aaron in June 1993.

His sessions with the GAL-appointed psychologist appear to focus on the monster or what happened on January 6, 1993. A three-year-old has difficulty remembering what he ate at lunchtime or what he did the day before. I do have trouble believing Aaron could remember what happened six months ago. I think that Aaron is playing make-believe because his stories change from looking out a window to being in the yard to elsewhere, what he saw the night of January 6, 1993. His dad drove his mom and her car into the lake to bury her in the backyard or elsewhere. Perhaps he is even repeating a story he heard. The foster father's friend hurt himself with a gun and threw it in a river. Police did find a gun in the river. Aaron said Mike threw it, but it was not his dad's gun, but his foster father's friend's gun. Even when we don't think children can hear us, they can. They love to repeat what they hear adults or older children say. A psychologist should know this fact. The psychologist asks during the sessions, "Remember when?". Aaron states that he does not remember the night of January 6, 1993, today. Where do all these stories come from that are in error?

In September 1993. The psychologist's notes state that Aaron started wetting the bed. He made statements that he was going to live with his dad again. He wanted to live with his dad. Then again, he starts saying that the monster is Daddy. He also stated that the monster was a different individual. This doesn't make any sense to me. It does suggest that Aaron may need to consult with another psychologist. Someone who was not always asking leading questions or questions that indicated that he saw Daddy hurt Mommy.

At this time, the judge permitted overnight visits with Bob and me. It would be permissible for us to state that if Aaron asks about his mother, we would say, "We do not know what happened to Mommy". GAL/CPT objected to Bob and me having custody of Aaron because we do not believe Mike killed Bonnie. Yet, they do not have a crime scene, a body, or any evidence that Mike harmed Bonnie.

Aaron began attending public school in the fall of 1993. He appears to be happy, and his cousin is accompanying him. The school records indicate that he is a good student and has presented no problems. His teachers have had nothing but positive remarks on his report card.

On October 6, 1993, we were in court for the Dependency of Aaron filed by Guardian Ad Litem and Child Protection Team. The judge said it was based on the facts of the case:

1. That there was a closely bonded relationship between Bonnie and her son, making it unlikely that she would voluntarily leave him for an extended period of time. (I go along with that. The keyword is voluntary. That would include, for Aaron's safety)

2. Bonnie was last seen on January 6, 1993, and has made no contact with family, friends, or her son since that time. (Correct>)

3. That her automobile, which she was driving when last seen, was discovered in the long-term parking section of the International Airport on January 7, 1993. (I agree.)

4. That her purse was found in a dumpster a couple of miles from the airport on January 7, 1993. (I agree>)

5. That her purse was undisturbed, that nothing was missing, and that it still contained her credit cards and a large quantity of cash. (It depends on what is called a large quantity of money. Annie stated it was

$1,500 when it was actually $150. The $1500, yes, but the $150 not so much.)

6. That Bonnie had plans which remain unfulfilled to this date, as evidenced by the lease application she signed at an apartment complex, in which she listed herself as separated from her husband and noted that she would be living in the apartment with her son, and as further evidenced by the quantity of money she had given to her friend to hold which remains unclaimed. (The plans remain unknown. She collected the deposit the next day without Annie and told me that she did not want Aaron in Orange Park and did not go to any daycare facilities for Aaron to change. The sum of money she supposedly gave to her friend, I have never seen a report on the amount Bonnie gave, nor a receipt of the amount in a police report, nor a statement by Bonnie's friend. Where is the evidence?)

7. The court is persuaded by the two separate statements made by the child and introduced into evidence, the first of which was the statement made to Bree of the Child Protection Team on January 8, 1993, and the second to his psychologist nine months later. The court finds that the two statements are internally consistent and that they comprise an eyewitness account of the child of the father shooting his mother. (You have got to be kidding me!! There is no audio or video of Aaron saying those statements, and two professionals stated that the abuse was unfounded and closed the case. Bree's statements are hearsay. Aaron was three years old and could not remember exactly where and when certain events happened. Aaron made other

statements that happened to his mother by his father that could not have occurred, as well as the father shooting his mother. There is no evidence to indicate there is a crime scene at Bonnie and Mike's home. There is no evidence that Bonnie did not leave on her own. Her car had no real evidence of foul play.) Another psychologist stated that Aaron was not traumatized. The school records indicate that the child is well-adjusted.

8. The court is equally impressed by the physical evidence, which established that the last person to drive Bonnie's automobile, and thereby the person who parked it in the long-term parking lot wore a Nike Air Advantage, size 10, shoe. Mike wore a size 10.... (The partial shoe print was on the back driver's side floorboard, which shows Mike may have gotten groceries or Aaron out of the car. The sand material in the shoe print could have come from a 60-mile or more radius. However, an eyewitness stated that she saw Bonnie and an older woman standing beside Bonnie's car at around 4:00 on January 7, 1993. Twenty minutes later, the women were gone, and Bonnie's emergency lights were flashing. That evidence fits the details of when and where Bonnie and her car were. Mike was being interviewed for a segment that was on the television news. This preponderance of evidence proves Mike was not responsible for Bonnie's disappearance.

9. Finally, the court stated that Mike did not appear to be a grieving husband. (What does a grieving husband look like? Especially when there is not enough evidence to show she was harmed, but enough to show she was still alive, and needed to be

found before she might be hurt. The police were looking for a body. Mike and his family were looking for a living person. Mike and Bonnie's parents put out a different flyer.

By all this baloney, Mike was ruled an abusive father physically, mentally, and emotionally. Aaron was adjudged a dependent child on October 27, 1993.

The supervisors of the safe house where the visits took place said that Bob and I were spoiling Aaron. It seems that we gave Aaron too much candy and presents. That is the way we are with all our grandchildren. Especially my husband. They find fault with all and everything we do. We tried to be honest in our dealings with everyone involved in this case. It was difficult when anyone is dealing with finding a loved one, fighting to have visitation rights, and trying to defend ourselves. We felt that we were not a rightful party and had no right to protect ourselves.

It seems GAL and CPT were trying to take visitation rights away from Mike, his parents, Bob, and me. They were ordering hearings on everything they could think of. They did not care what this was doing to Aaron's well-being. If he was upset after a visitation, it was because he did not want to see us, instead of the fact that he wanted to go home with his father, where he could visit all of us. How much could a toddler understand? What was negative, unbelievable, or positive, and what he should believe about why he could not go home to his dad? Aaron was not able to process all of what was happening in such a short period of time at three years old.

Chapter Six:
More Deceptions

"There is a price for speaking the truth. There is a bigger price for telling a lie."

Cornel West

On October 19, 1993, Bob and I went to Gail Billing's house. We called and left a message that we would be there at 9:00. We arrived to be met by a police officer. He told us to go. Gail did not want to talk to us, our lawyer, or our PI. I wanted to cry. After so many of her relatives told me she had information for us about Bonnie. To be shut down by the police seemed inconceivable. I decided to write to her.

I did not hear from Gail; however, our PI was finally able to talk to Gail. She said she saw Bonnie and an older woman standing beside Bonnie's car at around 4:00 in the long-term airport parking lot on January 7, 1993. Twenty minutes later, they were gone, but the emergency flashers were flashing on her car. The police knew this. They knew that Bonnie had her car keys and was alive. There was no need to put Aaron through all the trauma and abuse they were putting him through.

Gail worked for Budget Rent-A-Car, was a good and reliable citizen, and they interviewed her several times. I was told she even took a polygraph test. The police stated that all the people who claimed to have seen Bonnie on January 7th were not reliable or were unsure of what they observed. However, they believed two people who were proven to be unreliable. They changed their story and continued to lead the investigation. Mike's parents were unreliable. We were unreliable. Friends were unreliable. Most, if not all, of these individuals were proven to be outstanding citizens.

When Bob and I were asked to tell our feelings about Bonnie's disappearance, only what the police wanted to share with the public was aired. Only the negative or people who felt Mike was guilty of harming Bonnie were aired. Bob and I kept trying to find political or influential people to at least listen to the information and evidence that created doubt about whether Mike did not fit the picture painted by Annie, Bennie, and the police. When we thought we had found an individual, they were dismissed from helping us. They were moved horizontally or vertically, and they could not work with us.

At the end of 1993, "Someone" came up with the idea of a memorial service for Bonnie. That was another punch in the gut for us. There was still no evidence of a violent crime or proof that Bonnie left for some unknown reason. However, family members and even some members of the Church felt that a memorial service would be appropriate. Bob and I, as well as Mike and his family, did not attend. We could not submit to the fact that Bonnie was dead when we were still looking for a living person. A memorial service would be saying, Stop looking for a living person.

The memorial service was held at the Industrial Tradeport near the International Airport. It would have been an honorable memorial if all the facts were truthful and plausible. We could not give in to the speculation of false information and overwhelming facts that Bonnie was alive on January 7, 1993. We could not condemn Mike for something we knew he could not have done.

The newspaper articles stated that Annie was an aunt. She was not to Bonnie. It stated that the family was on opposite sides. Bob and I did not consider the family as being on opposite sides. We had different opinions; however, we didn't stop talking to or loving each other. We were family and always would be.

Aaron's guardians from the GAL were being changed. Our oldest daughter was unable to care for Aaron. Just as Bonnie knew it was too much to ask her to care for Aaron in 1992. She had too much on her plate to care for another small child. We were glad that at least one of our daughters was able to care for Aaron. I had Power of Attorney papers to care for Aaron. Bonnie had a will made on the same date as the Power of Attorney paper, notarized by Annie. The Will stated that I was to care for Aaron if, for some reason, Mike was unable to care for him.

One of the hold-ups for me was Aaron's caregiver's involvement with the psychologist. Bob started working out of state as a consultant. The psychologist seemed to have problems with a telephone conference with Bob. She also had difficulties meeting with Bob on Fridays or Mondays.

Finally, on March 17, 1994, after much objection from GAL, the judge ruled that it was in Bob's and my best interest to care for Aaron. Of course, it did not take long for GAL to find a reason to object to something they disapproved of and bring about another hearing.

One of the things they disapproved of was letting Mike call Aaron at bedtime. Aaron was so excited about his dad calling. He smiled and laughed the whole phone call. He went right to sleep and slept well. What could be wrong with that? GAL thought it was detrimental for that to take place. Aaron could hardly wait for his dad to call. It seemed more detrimental to take away that privilege for Aaron and Mike. When it showed the love and bond between them, how could they take it away? I guess that is why it showed the love and bond Aaron and Mike had for each other.

When Aaron first arrived, one of the first things he told me was that he had been told that he would be living with me forever. I was happy, but I knew how determined the opposing force was not to let that happen. We were in a good routine. He liked going to work at the same school as our youngest daughter. I could not believe an adult would tell a child something they knew might not be true, given what had transpired thus far.

Aaron's psychologist advised that no telephone calls take place. Doctor Kropp advised that even further psychological therapy was not necessary. There were no post-traumatic issues. He saw no reason to take him from his family. Why was one therapist's findings the right choice? It was driving a wedge between Aaron and those he loved by not allowing any visitations or phone calls from his dad.

Aaron was on his fourth Guardian Ad Litem in a year. At the last hearing regarding the phone calls, nothing was mentioned about our son, who has just turned 18. This became an issue after we signed papers not to pursue suing the state over Aaron. My husband and I were unaware of the legal implications of what that meant. Our lawyer said it was done in good faith. That was a big mistake.

Our appeal for custody of Aaron was turned down:

1. Because we used bad judgment in having a son who supposedly stole firearms and stored them on our property. The police were at our home twice with no warrants, stating that Robbie had stolen guns and stored them in our garage. The first time Bob was not home, I let them search the garage. Nothing found. The second time Bob was home. He asked if they had a search warrant. They said no. He told them to come back when they did. Robbie was never charged or even questioned. That was a bogus reason not to regain custody.

2. The next accusation was partially true; however, no charges were made. Bob and I were out of town, and Robbie decided to have a party. The house was a big

mess. Robbie claimed the house had been robbed. The doors were not kicked in, and yes, a few things were missing that I treasured, but they were not expensive. I just had a mess to clean up.

3. We used poor judgment in allowing our son to live in his home. At that time, he had a job and lived in another house. He did not come home again to live and married his girlfriend. They had two children who were never taken from them.

4. We never would have had to choose between Aaron and our son to live with us. Our son decided before the hearing that he would live elsewhere. Robbie was never a threat to anyone, least of all a child.

It was ruled that Aaron would continue as a foster child. It was unbelievable. Even visitation was eliminated. How could people whose main job is to protect and do what is in the child's best interest make the kind of decisions these people have made?

We had no idea what we were supposed to do, what Aaron was feeling, or what would happen. Mike was trying to comply with what HRS and the court wanted to do, but it seems he could not do enough.

My heart cried out for us all. I didn't know what to pray for anymore. I just knew God was the only one who could help us get through it. At this point, the hurt, pain, and anguish were ever-present. We were still looking for Bonnie and doing what we could to get Aaron home. Both seemed impossible at this time due to a lack of support legally and from the police department.

Aaron's foster parents have reported that Aaron is happy, playful, has a good appetite, sleeps well, and joins in family activities. Is this behavior that of a child who has been traumatized? It seems more like the behavior of a child with a well-adjusted upbringing. The behavior Dr. Kropp described to Aaron during their interview. Perhaps another independent psychologist's report is needed to determine the best course of action for Aaron.

The foster mother said that Aaron has feelings of separation anxiety when anyone leaves. Under the circumstances, for his age and past experiences, I believe that sounds normal. It has been almost a year and a half since Bonnie, his mother, left, and he has been struggling to get by. He does not know what will happen next. He demonstrated resilience and a willingness to adapt to change.

Interviews with the new guardian in April 1994 were reported well with an open-minded viewpoint. She stated how we felt and what we thought needed to be done. Her interview with Aaron's psychologist reflected her feelings about us, which were exactly as we had stated. She was against any visitations with Aaron's dad and all grandparents. The doctor indicated that if Aaron asked to see any of us, she would grant visitation to resume. Of course, if conversations are avoided or the subject is changed quickly, Aaron would probably not ask.

We do not know what Aaron was told about why we did not visit or why the visits ended. Perhaps he was under the impression that we didn't care about him. One particular instance that makes me question why Aaron didn't talk about us happened when I was visiting my oldest daughter, and her two children told me that Aaron had said he loved me. I wanted to cry. I could hardly tell them I loved him, too.

There was another time when our oldest daughter said that Aaron wanted to make a book about his mother. She asked for pictures of his mom. The pictures could also include his dad and anyone else. How is that not asking about us and even his mother? I could no longer trust what the system said. I could not believe what they said about our grandson. We would never tell Aaron that we did not believe him, whatever he told us, even if he said Daddy killed Mommy. And we would not tell him that we knew she was alive or where she might be, or the negative feelings we have of Annie and Bennie. We would wait for the truth of what happened to Bonnie or factual evidence.

The month of May 1994 was brutal. The judge wanted Bob to come to court or face jail for contempt of court if he did not disclose where one of his contacts had indicated that Bonnie might be. He would not tell. It would put lives in jeopardy. We were filing for visitation rights with Aaron. We did not have any rights due to the findings in the last court session, and we signed a paper stating that we would not appeal/sue. What a travesty. Because of one biased doctor's opinion, we were ostracized from Aaron's life. My husband would have gone to jail to be heard about what the system was doing. They did not give him a chance. The contempt charge was dropped. We had no visitation rights.

Mike's dad was ordered to stop videotaping visitation sessions. The place of the visitations was also ordered to stop. Aaron's psychologist deemed it detrimental to Aaron. No professional cases were cited to justify the psychologist's therapy or objections to what Mike or the grandparents were doing. Where were the instances where visitations were taken entirely away, and were they beneficial for the child? The psychologist stopped taping Aaron's sessions. It infringed on Aaron's trust and privacy. She said Aaron may feel his confidentiality will be violated. We are talking about a four-year-old here. She has a hidden camera. What is she terrified of?

Bob wrote a press release:

A year and a half ago, I would not have believed I would find myself in this position. For months, I was quick to tell anyone who would listen to every piece of information I had seen. Then I realized that the "authorities" were not only not following up on leads identified, but they were actively suppressing information and isolating me from opportunities to search for my daughter. Police officials have recorded conversations and ordered people not to talk to me or my private investigator.

Unless every lead is followed up thoroughly instead of suppressed, it will jeopardize the conviction of anyone the police attempt to charge concerning my daughter's disappearance. I do not wish for an innocent person to be convicted, nor do I wish for a guilty person to be acquitted due to police errors of omission and commission.

The night security guard at the motel where my daughter's purse was found claims to have seen my daughter on the night of her disappearance. The police have decided to discredit his testimony by describing the security guard as "not playing with a full deck" and intimidated by family members who questioned him. It does not represent the value of a security guard.

The motel maintenance man identified a person who seemed very interested in the dumpster. This person was later picked up in another city for stalking a school teacher. When this person failed a polygraph test, the police here were notified to question him about our daughter. The police responded that we have our man.

A motel maid who claims to have seen my daughter was questioned several times by the police without weakening her conviction as to what she saw, and was finally able to sit with a sketch artist, who produced a sketch of a man who was allegedly accompanying my daughter. The police have not only failed to release the sketch, but they also deny its existence.

In my opinion, the authorities have tried to discredit every witness that I identified to them. The authorities have ordered witnesses to be silent.

An airport car rental employee who claims to have seen my daughter and a companion was ordered by the police not to talk to me, my wife, or my private investigator. When my wife and I arrived at this person's home, police officers were there, and my wife and I were asked to leave.

I want to find my daughter. "The authorities" will not help me and have hampered my efforts in the past. I will not allow the authorities to handicap my efforts any further.

Suppose there are people out there who have information, whether or not they have given it to the police. In that case, I ask that they provide that information for my attorney, Kathy Sands, or my private investigator, MG Detective Agency. We will act on that information and maintain Confidentiality.

Like many Americans, I have lost a lot of faith in and respect for "the system". The judge has elected to take this personally and find me in contempt of her court.

I feel that she is adding insult to the injuries and losses I have sustained over the last 18 months.

The end of the press release that did not transpire was unfortunate. It would have been beneficial to have been able to give it to the press; however, I doubt the police would have allowed it to be printed or aired on the news.

In August 1994, I decided to return to school and pursue a degree in special education. I needed to start thinking forward. There have been so many setbacks. We seem to be unable to win any battles in court. Even when we did find a different child psychologist who said Aaron's psychologist was mistreating Aaron's diagnosis, she should not be taking visitations away. Her strong recommendation was to find a new therapist.

We thought "Unsolved Mysteries" would help us out. At the end of the airing, we were greatly disappointed. They did what the police dictated. Bob and I were the grieving parents and the only ones who did not believe Mike killed Bonnie. I could not believe this was happening! What would it take for people's eyes to be opened? We were supposedly not friendly to our children. We were still close to them. They knew we loved them.

We were still under a gag order, not allowed to discuss Aaron or the case we were fighting, not even with each other. We were fighting to become a "party" and start visitation rights. We were trying to fight for Bonnie's rights as a parent. They were trying to take away her paternal rights. Even though she was supposedly dead, the court was saying she had abandoned Aaron. I suppose Bonnie's Power of Attorney and Will, which gave me the authority to care for Aaron, did not hold any weight. Of course, they took my rights away first. Then they were taking away Bonnie's rights.

Mike was trying to help a girl out, and they became more than just friends. The police notified us that Mike let this girlfriend wear Bonnie's clothes, which were too small for her. Another tactic is to produce anger towards Mike. We may have felt upset, but we realized he had his wife and son taken from him for over a year. Mike did ask us a while back to take whatever we wanted from Bonnie's. I never thought it would take this long before the details of Bonnie's disappearance took place.

Since we are non-parties, we cannot file motions or do much of anything. I feel this is insane! How can we be non-parties when it is our daughter and grandson? Even having two professional psychologists say Aaron's psychologist is wrong did not change the police, CPT, GAL, or the judge's mind. We could not even receive help from organizations, politicians, or anyone else who might help. What is wrong? We were not given a reason, just sorry, we cannot help you.

Aaron's psychologist wanted pictures of us individually. We were skeptical at first. We did send them through our attorney. After receiving the pictures, she said she hoped that Aaron would say he wanted to see us. She would then talk about visitation once again.

In the court session on October 13, 1994, Aaron's psychologist said that she had no specific diagnosis for Aaron. She was treating symptoms. She had no idea when Aaron would have to be treated. She said that Aaron's behavior became disruptive at home when visitations began. (That was strange that the school did not report any behavior problems.) She said she lost our trust when we allowed Mike to call Aaron. (The phone calls were approved in a court order. This should not have been an issue with the psychologist.) Aaron's psychologist's last statement was that she believed foster care was best for Aaron.

Dr. Kropp testified using chapter and verse about Aaron's symptoms and said Aaron had a "detachment syndrome". Which meant he needed to be with family/Mike. His statements did receive the judge's attention.

The judge stated that she was in favor of a controlled restoration of family visits. She wanted to see Aaron. On October 18, 1994, Family visitation was again restored. All seemed to be going well between all parties, and visitations began in December 1994. Then, an emergency hearing was set for December 15. The police want to stop Mike and his parents' visitations. The issue is that the State Attorney's office is not a party. The judge was moved to a lower court. Another judge was appointed. A new court date was set for January 12, 1995. We were told our visits went well. Our visitation rights during this court hearing were not about us. We did not attend, nor did our lawyer.

Another one of those "tripped over a tree trunk and landed on our faces".

Chapter Seven:
Our Son and His Wife

"The dead cannot cry out for justice. It is a duty for the living to do so for them."

Lois McMaster Bujold

"My son was an epileptic. He had grand mal seizures. He had the wrong friends and ended up being at the P-Farm (jail for juveniles and non-violent offenders) a few times since he turned fifteen for breaking into cars, but not stealing the vehicles. He would steal stereo and/or speaker systems, cigarettes, and items left on seats that they could use. When he was almost 18, he was doing well, staying out of trouble. He had a girlfriend and a job. One night, he and his girlfriend were out, and she decided she wanted out of the car. She acted like she was going to jump out. He pulled over to let her out. He decided to drive around the block and pick her up. Walking around alone was not the best part of town for a girl. When he pulled up to her, she would not get back in his car. At that time, there was a lot of yelling back and forth. Someone called the police, thinking our son was up to no good. The police came, put my son in cuffs, and put him in the police car. I am not sure what transpired next; however, I know that his girlfriend yelled at the police that Robbie had seizures. That he was an epileptic. The officers seemed to be talking loudly to Robbie, and Robbie was talking loudly to them. Robbie put his foot through the police car window. Unhappy officers opened the car door and pulled him out. His head hit the sidewalk. Now, whether Robbie was having a seizure and the police officers were holding him down, or if the officers rubbed his face in the broken glass from the window. It was never in the police report, but his face was severely cut with glass embedded in his face. Robbie spent over five hours in surgery and had to call in a plastic surgeon to save his eye. Robbie decided to plea bargain to a felony and six months in the work release program—hardly the sentence of a violent offender. Perhaps if we had known all the facts of what happened, we could have had the felony taken off. Robbie paid for that until he passed at the age of 42. His wife died a year and a half later in a car accident.

Since this last arrest put us into another can of worms. We now had a felon living in our house. Our son's arrest made it easier for the GAL/CPT to suggest that we were unfit to care for Aaron. There probably would have been something else brought up that would have developed into the same scenario.

Chapter Eight:
What We Were Ruled to Believe

"Honesty is more than not lying. It is truth-telling, truth-speaking, truth-living, and truth-loving."

James E. Faust

The court hearing that our lawyer said was just about visitation rights for Mike's parents, not us. We did not need to be at this court hearing. Our lawyer would not be going. This was on December 21, 1994. The Sheriff and the State Attorney were parties to this hearing. The new Judge did not seem to care about what the previous judge had ruled or what had transpired at the last hearing. All visitations were taken away to visit Aaron. Bob did attend the hearing on January 12, 1995; however, he was late and was denied entry to the hearing. Our lawyer ordered a rehearing. Nothing is changing. The new judge sees the same picture that the police, GAL/CPT, and Aaron's psychologist have been painting since day one. No mention was made of two other psychologists, nor was any objective evidence presented.

On March 24, it was ruled that since Bob and I cannot support an acceptance of Aaron stating that Daddy hurt Mommy, we are denied custody and visitation rights. There would not be any change in the people caring for Aaron or any visitation rights for Aaron's father or other grandparents. Visitation would only commence if Aaron asked to see his grandparents. The new Judge would not hear of our pleas or any on behalf of Mike and his parents. The judge, on March 29, became insulting, saying things that were not true and providing no evidence to support his claims. Bob and I stood up and walked out.

Mike was still fighting for his paternal rights. He was doing all that the court and HRS asked him to do. HRS's goal was for the reunification between Aaron and his father. No matter what he did, it was never enough for GAL/CPT. He lost his paternal rights. Not long after, Aaron's foster parents adopted him.

The only ones who had a right to see Aaron were our oldest daughter and her family. No family members on Mike's side were allowed to see Aaron. That meant Annie and Bennie were not supposed to be able to see Aaron!

On April 18, 1995, Aaron's two cousins told Bob and me that Aaron misses us. We told them we miss him, too. It was so difficult not to say or do something to try to go see Aaron. We ran out of options. We fired our lawyer. We just tried to live for the sake of living and caring for the rest of our family.

Bob went on to be a self-employed engineering consultant. I went on to receive a master's degree in education for students with varied exceptionalities and worked in the public education system. Bob and I worked hard at our jobs and communicated with our family, except when talking about Aaron. Mike lost his parental rights. Mike and his family moved out of state to escape the gossip and negative feelings. I could not move away. If there was a chance Bonnie came home, I wanted to be where she could find us.

Is this the end of the story? No!!

I still wrote letters, trying to get someone to listen to the injustice that had been done. It was to no avail. I tried to find a lawyer to listen and give me a way to I could see the truth or expose a reason for Bonnie to disappear. How could I do that when the police would not consider investigating Annie and Bennie? Again, I had no way to become a party.

I would have given up, but the lies about Bonnie's disappearance were too hard for me to stop trying. I never felt alone. God held me up. I read scriptures, held Church callings, and attended church almost weekly. I did not find anyone that I could openly talk to about the events of Bonnie's disappearance, except God. I could talk to Bob; however, he would become upset. He felt he had failed Bonnie. He was supposed to protect her, but he did not know how.

In the fall of 1999, Bob started having health issues. He had put on weight, which added to his health problems. He did not want to see a doctor about his recurring problem of being out of breath. He finally could not help it, and a friend took him to the hospital. The doctors said he had a heart attack and had to have surgery. He was working on a project in New York. I flew up to be with him. His friends helped me find his apartment. The doctors had already set up the surgery for a couple of days after I arrived. The doctors were not optimistic about Bob's outcome. Bob had five bypasses done. He lived and was ready to leave the hospital a week after the surgery. The doctors weren't happy about this. They told him he needed a defibrillator. They had to convince him to undergo the procedure. Bob finally had that done, and a few days later, we drove home. He recuperated for six months doing things around the house. He was getting bored and wanted to go back to work.

There were many consulting jobs for him to do. People knew how skilled he was at his job and paid him well for his efforts. He was known for his honesty, hard work, and punctuality. Work kept his mind off his inability to help Bonnie and not being able to see Aaron, and it boosted his confidence in himself. I still wrote letters, taught my special students, and assisted my school with various tasks when requested. That kept me going. I was helping my mom, who lived sixty miles away, on Saturdays. I helped a friend with disabilities. I did not lack for things to do. My husband and I kept busy, but we did make time for each other and our children. God helped to keep our commitment to each other. I still had inspiration that led me to information about events from Aaron's case that seemed to go nowhere. The information brought back memories or kept the memories fresh in my mind. This later helped me piece the information together, but not all of it. We were unable to obtain some of the necessary information. We were not attorneys to extract some key information.

In December of 2014, things started to change. Bonnie and Mike's home was now Aaron's. The renters who had been living in the home had moved out. Aaron decided to renovate the inside and outside of the house. The first thing he wanted to do was to tear out the swimming pool. Aaron had friends who were willing to help him do that. While demolishing the pool, Aaron found something that looked like a coconut. He picked it up and realized it was a skull. He put it back where he found it and called the authorities.

The remains were found near a shower, a water fountain, and water pipes connecting the house and the swimming pool. The water fountain had been removed years earlier. The old, rotten wood floor in the shower was removed years earlier by a renter. In pictures taken at the time of Bonnie's disappearance, grass and pool chlorine jugs were sitting by the shower. They appeared to be undisturbed.

The remains were also located close to the house and directly adjacent to the pipes. It seems that with a shower and water fountain there in 1993, it would have been challenging to bury someone. The bones were not all together; they were in a construction-type bag with a smaller pink bag inside. They did not say or could not identify what was in the pink bag. The construction bag had roots growing through it, which were not recognized as to the type of trees or bushes. I thought this was strange because I had placed bags under mulch next to trees and bushes, and after ten years was able to pull them up and reuse the bags for yard trash. With the house, pool, driveway, no close trees, and fencing, I would think the remains would be in better shape. There was also a layer of cement over the remains and under the bricks of the shower. The renter who changed the wood to bricks stated that he did not notice or put cement under the bricks. The dirt was not determined to be different from the surrounding dirt. This was important to determine if the body had been previously moved from being buried elsewhere.

The police came to our house and said there was nothing to identify and that we could come down and look, but there was nothing to identify but the skull. We decided not to look at the skull. They were going to do a DNA test to determine the identity. Bob and I felt that there was no way the remains could be those of Bonnie. They did not ask for our DNA.

In a police report, they had talked about taking DNA from our daughters, but never did. In 2009, they did take DNA from Aaron; however, they never used it to identify the remains. Mike requested another DNA test to be conducted. Bob and I requested another DNA test to be conducted. Mike's lawyer said it wasn't necessary, and all agreed it was Bonnie's remains. I do not know who everybody was! After the trial, we learned that Mike and his parents all wanted another DNA test to be done. The DNA retest was never done. All we know is that it was a Caucasian woman of European descent. That leaves much to learn about who exactly the remains are. The dental records did not completely match. Her dental records stated that she had a healthy, well-maintained mouth and teeth.

Many bones were missing. However, all 10 acrylic fingernails were found, and the rings that Annie described in 1993 were also found when the remains were found. They did not ask me for descriptions of her rings or fingernails at any time. I wrote about them in my first book. She would not have been wearing the panda ring or the Gator ring at that time. She took those rings off as soon as she got home from work. It was not a blue sapphire ring but an emerald or green ring with a diamond on each side that was given to her for her eighteenth birthday. Her birthstone.

The clothes that the remains had on were not Bonnie's size. We were not aware of the clothes and rings before the trial. We were not aware of many of the details beforehand, prior to the trial. Again, we were treated as nonparties. Annie and Bennie were treated as more than Bonnie's parents, best friends, or close relatives when they were none of these.

Cadaver dogs were used in the search of Bonnie and Mike's house, in searches in 1993, and again in 1996 when the police received an anonymous letter about Bonnie being buried in the backyard. This is a clear indication that the remains were not there in 1993 or 1996. Since Mike and his family did not live in Jacksonville, Mike never returned, and John only came back to address the renter's problems. So, who put the remains where they were found?

The local newspaper on August 26, 2015, stated that the State Attorney and the lead detective (who was now the state attorney investigator) would put together the 20-some years of individual circumstances to put in front of a jury to seek "justice for Bonnie"—the title of my first book. Individual circumstances do not sound like evidence. I thought the evidence was what you needed for a conviction. That does sum up what they had, along with hearsay.

They could have provided evidence if they had checked the Sunshine Inn records for the night Curt and Bonnie were supposedly having their affair, and examined the time more closely when Bonnie's car drove into the airport's long-term parking lot. They really did have that information, and never reported it that I was able to find. The police should have done a complete DNA test to prove conclusively that it was Bonnie's remains. They should have been able to confirm the crime scene that Aaron described soon after she disappeared. They had no evidence that Aaron saw Mike do any harm to Bonnie in front of him; they had no proof that Aaron was abused in any way, shape, or form. The police did not produce any expert witness who could say the bullet found in the items by the remains came from Mike's gun, even though they did have the fired bullets from Mike's guns. The police never had any objective evidence in the case against Mike. I should say they had or should have had.

Mike's attorney should have produced expert witnesses who could have stated that Mike could not have put the body where it was found. The fired bullet did not come from any of Mike's guns. The attorney could have proven that Aaron's testimony was hearsay, and no crime scene was ever found that Aaron ever described. The attorney had two other written reports that Arron suffered from detachment syndrome rather than post-traumatic syndrome. It could have been essential to know why he was still seeing a psychologist. The two other psychologists said treating Aaron with post-traumatic stress disorder could cause other psychological problems in the future. Mike's attorney could have raised doubt in the jury's minds that Bonnie was still alive on January 7, 1993.

Many circumstances suggest that the police had not been compiling evidence or were inept as investigators. Perhaps they were paid to go along with the bad guys. Perhaps they were instructed by their superiors on what they wanted to happen in this unsolved case. It ruined many lives. The authorities became the abusers.

Justice for Bonnie was not served. She left many clues as to why she left. The clues went unheeded.

Chapter Nine: Bonnie's Clues

"Delay of justice is injustice."

Walter Savage Landor

You may ask, "What clues did Bonnie leave to indicate why she left?'

The pills she left in her purse were the first clue. In May of 1992, Mike asked me why Bonnie was so unhappy and mentioned that the girls in her office might be passing pills to one another. Annie may or may not have known. I told Bonnie if that was true, she should consider what the pills could do to her mind and body. Maybe she would be happier without the pills. When the pills were in her purse, it seemed to tell me that I was right, and she saved her portion as proof.

Leaving her purse in the dumpster with money and credit cards, she was saying I was not robbed, I just left. Professional doctors, especially psychologists, would say this was a fact, if they had been asked! The purse was placed so that it would be found. If we had the testimony of the person who was watching the dumpster until after the police arrived, we might have discovered who placed the purse in the dumpster.

Parking her car next to the road with the flashers on indicated she wanted the car found fast. I do not believe the mess inside the vehicle was made by Bonnie or the ones she was with. It does not fit the pattern. Hearsay about the mess was that Bennie had created it looking for Bonnie's keys and a police radar that he had bought for Bonnie. The seat being in a position that was not customary for Bonnie could have been because she did not drive the car to the airport. Gail Billings stated that Bonnie was with an older woman who could have driven the vehicle. The car keys were never found. This indicated that the last person driving the vehicle kept the car keys. They may have thought about retrieving the car. It was parked in the long-term parking area. The parking lot attendants stated that the car was not parked there before 3:00 a.m. on January 7, 1993. This means Bonnie was not murdered on January 6, 1993.

If Bonnie's two friends from high school and work were deposed, we may have learned more facts about Bonnie's real feelings and what may have transpired at work before she disappeared. We may have learned when or if she was having an affair. I only have hearsay about that. Of course, the police reports and the limited investigation tell me the affair was not factual. Curt testified that he only did what the police asked him to do. Why would the police ask him to do anything but tell the truth? The police could have had facts by checking motel records.

When Bonnie came to our house at the end of 1992, she went to Aaron's room, where he slept when he stayed overnight. She sat on the bed and said, "So this is Aaron's room". I said it was also, and named our other grandchildren when they spent the night. Bonnie said it in a strange way, but that is what she meant. It just indicates to me that Bonnie felt Aaron was going to be living with me!?

During this time, Bonnie said that she did not want Aaron in Orange Park. Annie and Bennie live there. She would not have been looking for an apartment or a daycare in Orange Park. She was also taking Aaron to my school's functions when I was unable to attend. Another indication to me that she would like Aaron to live with me and go to the school where I work.

In November 1992, Bonnie granted me power of attorney and a will that gave me custody of Aaron in the event of her death or if Mike was unable to care for Aaron for any reason. Bonnie also had a Profit-Sharing Plan that I was a beneficiary of if Mike could not claim. I do not have the date of this transaction. Why would Bonnie go through the trouble of creating these three legal documents if she wanted our oldest daughter to have custody of Aaron a day after she supposedly made another will, dated the day before the power of attorney and will, which gave me custody of Aaron, if Mike could not care for Aaron? There appears to be a signature difference. The forms I received were different from the ones the lawyers used. Annie notarized the ones for me. The will with custody of our daughter was written by Bennie and Annie's lawyer. The date of March 27, 2003, was on the cover page of this will. What is the truth?

Bonnie was looking for a new job at the end of 1992. She told me how upset she was with Annie and Bennie. She would have rather worked for a dead-end job than for them. Why did she continue? Whatever the reason seemed to be, it was causing her unhappiness. So much so that she did not want to share with her parents the reason for her anxiety.

Bonnie was identified in too many places on January 7, 1993, to be a coincidence or not to give consideration that she might be alive. She seemed to make it known that she was alive and was not in danger. She had no doubt that Mike had done anything to her. Annie and Bennie seemed to want the police and all to believe that Mike had killed Bonnie from the very first moment her purse was found. Why would they want their nephew to be accused of killing Bonnie? Annie wanted everyone to believe she was a close relative and Bonnie's best friend. Annie made too many mistakes, as noted by professionals, to be believed. The police seemed to accept her every word without any evidence being brought forward. The police kept "evidence" suppressed that proved Mike could not have killed Bonnie and that she may still be alive.

I accidentally hit a stand on which a porcelain doll was sitting and broke the doll's leg. It dawned on me that this was one of the last things Bonnie, Ginny, my youngest daughter, and I had done together. In September 1992, Bonnie signed us up to make porcelain dolls at a friend of ours' shop. We had to complete the dolls by the end of November, when our friend was closing her shop. That would be between Ginny's and my birthdays. I did collect dolls, but not this type. Bonnie seemed to want to do this, so Ginny and I said yes. Bonnie seemed to be stressed for time; however, she seemed to enjoy it more than Ginny and me. I forgot about it with so many other pressing matters to attend to. I treasure that memory more now. I couldn't believe that it had been pushed back or set aside. That is how thoughtful Bonnie was about the simple details that mean a great deal. Just like the "Power of Attorney" and Will being done in November. She seemed to have everything set for her disappearance.

Chapter Ten:
The Murder Trial
Or
Travesty of Justice

"Truth is powerful and it prevails."

Sojourner Truth

We parked as close as we could get to the courthouse. Bob wasn't doing great, and we had the courthouse steps to contend with. We met with the state attorneys representing the state in a pretrial conference room. The attorney who had been in charge of the case since 1993 and had prepared for this trial had been called on duty elsewhere. Or could it have been because he had revealed important information to me about Bonnie's car keys? They were not to be found and were never found. No one was supposed to know that key piece of information.

When it was time to enter the courtroom, we did not rush in. We sat on the side where all our family and those who held Mike accountable for Bonnie's death. We were not seated in the first row or the second row. We were sitting in the fourth row. Again, it appeared we were not close relatives!? I was given a chair to sit in the aisle because of my hearing problem, not to make a significant difference in how easy it is for me to hear.

Between sessions, we communicated with Mike's parents and his relatives, and their friends. Aaron even talked to us. Aaron stated that he did not remember anything that happened in 1993. He said that he did read my book, No Justice for Bonnie. He believed parts of it but would not commit to what he did or did not believe. I did not even ask. He sat on a bench outside the courtroom with an arm around me. He seemed to be telling me that he believed that I loved him, and he loved me. At least, no one denied that fact.

There was a growing complaint about Mike's assistant attorney saying disparaging remarks about knowing Mike was guilty. She should have excused herself, and so should Mike's attorney if he felt the same. Mike deserved to be defended guilty or not. He was not defended. They should have at least presented the facts, even to the extent that there was no evidence to prove without a doubt that there was even a crime scene and that it was, in fact, Bonnie's body. Most of what the prosecution presented was hearsay and lacked sufficient evidence to prove that the events occurred. They could have had evidence, but did not obtain those facts.

There was little mention of using a cadaver dog. I was able to find over 25 pages of areas where they used cadaver dogs and infrared aerial to find a body covering from Bonnie and Mike's home to miles around. Nobody was ever found buried where they should not have been from 1993 to 1996.

The trial days dragged on, with no expert witnesses being called by Mike's attorneys. The police knew the body recovered had been moved. It was obvious to everyone. Yet, the defense never brought up that fact. The number of people who saw Bonnie alive on January 7, 1993, was another fact not disclosed, and it is likely that whoever drove the car to the long-term parking lot still had the key to Bonnie's car. There is still the question of a crime scene. The gun shell found was never proven to have come from Mike's gun, and the police had shells from Mike's guns. The alleged affair could have been proven if the motel Bonnie and Curt stayed at had been checked. The police records of the two Kurt's testimonies, one from 1993 and the one from the trial, would be proof that those facts had errors.

Where were Bonnie and Mike's friends? Why weren't they called by the prosecution or the defense? Something is strange about that! They should have been called to inform them of what happened at work and the last days Bonnie was present. Surely, they could have been deposed in 1993 to set the stage for what was going on at home and/or at work.

Aaron said he did not remember anything that happened in 1993. What he said years later does not fit any evidence.

Two psychologists deferred to the police appointed psychologist. Two psychologists said that Aaron should not have been taken away from his father and that it could cause him to have other problems in the future. What Aaron said that only the CPT interviewer could say he said amounts to hearsay. No proof was provided to prove that Arron said his dad hurt his mom.

The state had two inmates who said Mike told them he killed Bonnie. That is incredible. One did say after the trial that he lied. Mike has never said that to friends, family, a girlfriend, or his wife. Why would he say that to a stranger right before his trial? Not even close to believable. The state seemed to be grasping at straws, and the defense did not use the information in defending Mike.

The last insult to injury was that Bob and I could not be called as witnesses because what we had to say would be considered hearsay. If that weren't so ridiculous, it would have been funny. It was in a sick way.

Bob and I could not believe what transpired at this trial or travesty of justice. We were unable to stay for the final sentencing. It was so unreal and disgusting that it made us sick.

At least one of the jurists said they based their decision on Aaron's statement that Daddy hurt Mommy. Mike's attorneys should have had that ruled as hearsay and inadmissible as evidence. There was no audio or video presented, and Aaron said he does not remember anything that happened. The Jury should have based its judgment on the facts and actual evidence presented.

The one inmate rescinded his testimony that Mike had said anything to him about killing Bonnie after the trial. The other inmate's testimony lacked credibility. Mike lived twenty-five years without telling anyone about killing Bonnie, including friends, relatives, girlfriends, or anyone. Why would he say that to an inmate? Even the inmate's story conflicted with the evidence presented.

In Aaron's testimony, he did not have any memory of the night his mother left or even living with our oldest daughter. He was not even told why his dad or grandparents visited him. He did not know that if he said he wanted to see us, they were supposed to contact us, and visits would resume. Aaron must have felt we no longer cared about him. We just abandoned him. Aaron's statement sounds more like the two psychologists' statement of "detachment syndrome", not "post-traumatic stress disorder". It was also stated that Aaron was seeing his state-appointed psychologist for another issue involving his mental state. Still, we were not informed of the problem due to confidentiality. I understand that, however, the other two psychologists said he needed to be back with his family to help him deal with his mother's sudden absence, or this could develop into other psychological problems. I suppose we will not know all the answers. It would be nice to know some of the main questions.

Aaron's feelings about Annie have changed from January 6, 1993, to the present. That first day, he screamed and would not even stay in the same room she was in. He was never that way with his dad or grandparents, not even strangers. It shows how he trusted even strangers more than Annie. During Aaron's testimony, he showed little or no attachment to his dad or grandparents. Of course, he sat by Annie, Bennie, our oldest daughter, and others. The last family court session on who was to have contact with Aaron, Annie, and Bennie was not on that list. That gave me some hope that Bonnie was there. During court, it was brought up that Annie and Bennie only saw him twice a year. If that were so, they seemed to be very close at court time. They came and went together with Aaron and his wife, as well as Aaron's foster family. Aaron's wedding took place at Annie and Bennie's home.

Aaron stated in his deposition on June 9, 2016, what happened when he discovered the skull supposedly of his mother. Aaron explained that he was renovating his mom and dad's sold house. He began by demolishing the old swimming pool from the outside. He removed bricks where an old shower base was replaced by a renter from old slippery wood to brick. Aaron then came to a cement slab under the bricks that he thought the renter had poured to make the area level for placing the bricks. That was not the case. The renter stated that he did not install the cement slab. He did not know there was a cement slab. It seems unlikely that there was a cement slab when he put the bricks down. When Aaron broke the slab, he broke a pipe. He had to dig down to fix the leak. When he did, he saw what he thought was a coconut. He picked it up and realized it was a skull. Aaron said it was between six and twelve inches down from the slab. When he realized it was a skull, he put it back down where he had picked it up and called the authorities.

Aaron was a landscaper and was asked about the covering of the skull. He held only the top portion of the skull. It appeared that the covering of the skull extended from the top part to the part of the eye sockets to the back portion of the skull. It appeared that the covering of the skull was not plastic, fabric, or plant growth, but was stringy. I would say that that description was hair. Why wasn't DNA taken from the stringy growth? It would have given us a great DNA sample and maybe given us more details of how the remains died. What a waste of money and time for both the prosecution and the defense!

Chapter Eleven:
Life Went On

"Never be afraid to raise your voice for honesty and truth and compassion against injustice and lying and greed. If people all over the world...would do this, it would change the earth."

William Faulkner

During the time the remains were found and Mike's arrest, my mother's health became worse. I kept driving the 60 miles to her home more and more. She would not live with us or sell her house to move closer. Bob's health was not improving either. My mom passed right before Thanksgiving in 22014.

Our son passed suddenly from a heart attack on 27 May 1917. It was overwhelming for us all. He had a wife and two beautiful daughters. They were not young children; however, they were not fully capable of functioning as adults yet. It was a terrible loss to us all. The youngest stayed with my daughter and her husband, who lived close by. The oldest daughter stayed with her mom, who moved back to us. At times, she stayed with us to help her mom sort through what she needed to do. Janet had some health issues of her own that made it difficult for her to work any longer.

A month after my son passed, his wife, Janet's mother, passed. That did not help Janet and her girls' psychological lives at all. We all tried our best to help each other by supporting each other's individual needs. It took the stress of Mike's trial off our minds. We each had our own family matters to cope with, and our opinions differed on the disappearance of Bonnie. Although it may have caused us to be less unified, we moved forward.

Bob had another heart attack and had a new defibrillator and a pacemaker put in. That slowed him down a little more, but he still worked hard on Ronnie's farm and a few consulting jobs. He was starting to think it was time to quit working. He was unable to climb around the buildings to take notes on what needed to be done and when regarding machine maintenance. He had others do most of the climbing around. In 2019, he retired, and it was the time of Mike's trial for the murder of Bonnie.

I decided to write my first book about Bonnie's disappearance. I did not think I would publish it. I just wanted to bring the injustice to the attention of the police and others to stop the proceeding from going to trial. It did not seem to be working.

There wasn't much we could do to help Mike. The information and evidence were there for Mike's lawyer to compile. He was given money to call expert witnesses to prove Mike's innocence. He should have been able to win the case!? I even gave the lawyer Bob's notes with details that a jury should not have convicted Mike without a reasonable doubt. I believe it was a mistrial because there was no evidence, and it was based on hearsay.

The weeks that preceded Mike's trial were strenuous. At this time, Bob and I were retired. We were both helping our daughter, Ronnie, out on her not-for-profit farm. Bob was not able to do as much as he would have liked, but it was a big help to her. It helped to keep our minds off the upcoming trial. Ronnie was having a yard sale to raise some needed money.

Mike's girlfriend from 1995 to 1996 came with her mother. Not to buy anything but to have a conversation with me. I did not know what to expect her to say. I braced myself for what she might say. I knew she had not lived well, partaking of drugs. She started by saying she was sorry for what I had to go through. She said Mike was a help to her family. That he did not abuse her or talk about any abuse to Bonnie. I was shocked that she never insinuated that Mike was abusive to anyone. Obviously, he had tried to change her way of life. Her mother was not far away, but far enough so that she could not hear all of what was being said. Then, at the end of her visit, she revealed the real reason: she wanted to talk to me. She said, "You know Annie was just trying to help Bonnie. She was a good friend to Bonnie." I almost wanted to scream. I had to bite my lips together. She knew I did not believe what she said about Annie. She thought she needed to repeat it.

I could not get over what she said. I knew Annie must have put her up to coming and having a conversation with me. How could she even know Annie? I knew Mike could not have introduced her to Annie. Annie must have wanted me to doubt that she just wanted to find justice for Bonnie. Did she believe I could not remember what she had said about Bonnie and that Bonnie wanted to be away from her?

A week before Mike's trial, Bob and I were invited to meet with the State Attorney to discuss the upcoming trial. That was a change of pace. We had always been on opposing sides! We saw Annie and Bennie, Aaron, Aaron's foster mother, and her biological daughter, our oldest daughter, as well as the state attorney who had been on the case since 1993, and another state attorney. Not much new information was provided that we had not heard before. No one said too much before we left. Why were Annie and Bennie present??

The next day, Ronnie received a call from the State Attorney, who was taking the case to court, calling to ask for me. I was on the farm, but not close enough to take the call. He had called my daughter, Shelly, and she couldn't answer his question, so she gave Ronnie's phone number to get in touch with me. The question, "Where was Bonnie's car key? He had looked everywhere and could not locate her car key." He wanted me to call him as soon as possible. Ronnie told me, and I did not know whether to laugh or cry. The one question we asked from day three, and we never received an answer. That answered our question. Bonnie or the ones she was with had her car key. The one question that says she was alive on January 7, 1993.

I could not tell Bob. It was just too much, too late. Mike's lawyer should have known. If he did not know the police never had the keys, it was his fault. We tried to get him to gather the information, and thought he was a reasonable attorney. Smarter than we were about the law. Based on the information we received from our investigator, his investigator should have had even more information, given their greater access to police records and knowledge of how to retrieve information. The attorney did not appear to conduct any investigation from the outset. Several attorneys on the case should have realized that having the CPT's word that Aaron said "Daddy shot Mommy" was hearsay. With no crime scene or any evidence to support that Aaron said that, again, makes it hearsay.

Needless to say, Bob and I were trying to understand how this could have taken place in the history of our legal system. Our hands had been tied since the first year of Bonnie's disappearance. We had been shut out and cast aside. We just wanted justice and answers, but there was no way to achieve them. I should say, we did have answers, but no legal way to make them public. God gave me the answers and peace I needed to move forward. He still is.

With the sickness and deaths in the family, I could not put all the pieces and materials I had together. A year after my husband's death, I started putting my thoughts and material together. I thought I had only one last way to bring my husband and our story, our evidence, to light: write another book. The more I searched our material, the more facts I found. I had facts that I did not know where they came from. I found other ways to gain more information in this new tech world.

Chapter Twelve: Acquiring More Information

"You can't go back and change the beginning, but you can start where you are and change the ending."

C. S. Lewis

God was still helping gather information about this situation. Bob passed away on July 27, 2021. His health deteriorated after the trial. It was challenging to move forward as the family grew, with each child developing their own grandchildren and facing their own situations to deal with. Bob. I assisted our daughter, Ronnie, with the farm she had purchased. Then there was the pandemic to deal with. Bob pressed on doing what he could. In 2021, he did very little until July. He was in a wheelchair by then. He did not want to be hospitalized, which meant I had to watch him slowly pass. It broke my heart to have him leave this life; however, his suffering was over.

My son's daughter and her son, my great-grandson, came to live with me. It has been extra work, but rewarding. They help me, and I help them. After a year of grieving my husband, I started to think of all the mistakes made with Bonnie's disappearance. No, I could not undo the past. I had the option of doing what I did the year before the trial, writing about the experiences, good, bad, and ugly. In my first book, "No Justice for Bonnie," my point was to provide sufficient written information to hopefully prompt the police to reconsider and do the right thing, thereby avoiding a travesty of justice. That did not work and just gave them reasons not to make complete disclosures about the case. It prepared them on what to do and what not to do. One way to make sure Bob and I were not called to testify.

After a year of grieving, I started to look at all the information we had. I kept finding information I did not know we had or where it came from. Many people who could confirm or provide feedback had passed away. I received police reports and other records verified by the police, which helped fill in some missing information. Other records, including those from police and public records, helped.

Some documents that I passed on to Mike's lawyer, I was unable to retrieve. Most of the information I did find, I have already written about in this book.

The one fact that came up at the beginning of our investigation, and the one piece that put this case into perspective, is Bonnie's car key. The knowledge of where her car key was and why it was not in her car, or anywhere to be found, puts the knowledge of Gail Billings calling the police letting them know where Bonnie's car was and seeing Bonnie and another woman standing by the car at four o'clock in the afternoon of January 7, 1993 so important to solve the case. It means that Bonnie was alive. The people who reported seeing her at different establishments on January 7, 1993, are more believable and reiterate that Bonnie was a disappearance case rather than a homicide case.

WHY was Aaron subjected to abuse by the system?

Where were the checks and balances in our legal system that should have detected the inconsistencies that occurred from day one?

How could this case have taken over twenty-five years to be solved, given the number of real crimes involved?

I am still searching for justice for Bonnie and her family.

www.ingramcontent.com/pod-product-compliance
Lightning Source LLC
Chambersburg PA
CBHW041215130526
44582CB00024BA/11